Charlton Miner Lewis

The Foreign Sources of Modern English Versification

Charlton Miner Lewis

The Foreign Sources of Modern English Versification

ISBN/EAN: 9783744713962

Printed in Europe, USA, Canada, Australia, Japan

Cover: Foto ©ninafisch / pixelio.de

More available books at **www.hansebooks.com**

THE FOREIGN SOURCES

OF

MODERN ENGLISH VERSIFICATION.

WITH ESPECIAL REFERENCE

TO

THE SO-CALLED IAMBIC LINES OF 8 AND 10 SYLLABLES.

A THESIS PRESENTED
TO THE FACULTY OF THE GRADUATE DEPARTMENT
OF YALE UNIVERSITY,
UPON APPLICATION FOR THE DEGREE OF
DOCTOR OF PHILOSOPHY,

BY

CHARLTON M. LEWIS, B.A., LL.B.

BERLIN.
MAYER & MÜLLER.
1898.

PREFACE.

It was my original intention to offer a thesis on certain logical aspects of the theory of modern English verse, following lines suggested by Mayor's *Chapters on English Metre* and Bridges' *Milton's Prosody*. After considerable study, however, I found myself still in an embarassing uncertainty as to several of the most fundamental questions involved, and it was clear that a preliminary investigation of the historical origin of our verse-forms was indispensable. All the topics most intimately involved in this investigation have already provoked separate discussion, but there has never been any satisfactory coördination of results; and the lack of just this has led to many hasty inferences. The purpose of this paper is to trace the main line of descent of our modern versification, from the classical quantitative verse and the Old English accentual verse, through the various forms that were cultivated in mediæval Latin, English and French.

To carry such an investigation into all the topics usually treated under the head of versification, would of course be impracticable within the ordinary limits of a doctor's thesis. I have therefore limited myself as narrowly as possible to one topic,—the one that seemed to me most essential. I have disregarded all questions as to stanza-form, rime, alliteration, euphony of vowels, and the like, and considered only the internal mechanical structure of the individual verse. Even here, to avoid complication, I have for the most part confined my attention to the two types of iambic verse which prevail so conspicuously in English poetry;—choosing those two types not only because they are of the greatest literary importance, but also because the story of their evolution illustrates, in the most clear and straight-forward way, the principles which seem to me to control the development of verse. Moreover, as to certain matters which seemed to have been already argued thoroughly enough by others, I have given only the barest possible statement of facts. This will be found especially true of the matters covered in the last chapter,—intrinsically the most important part of the whole. Sievers seems almost to have said the last word about pure Old English versification, and Schipper, in observing the facts of Middle-English verse-development, has left nothing undone that was needed for my present purposes: and I have therefore contented myself, for the most part, with a brief and somewhat fragmentary review of their conclusions.

The terminology of the subject is very unsettled. I have used the words *arsis* and *thesis* in their original sense,—the former being marked in marching by raising the foot, the latter by setting it down. I have used the word *rhythm* in its ordinary sense, except where special reference to the so-called Latin "rhythms" is sufficiently indicated by the context, or by quotation-marks. The terms *iambic, trochaic,* etc., when applied to accentual verse, though not unobjectionable, are sanctioned by a fairly common usage, and are at least convenient. They are less illogical, too, than *rising* and *falling,* the best substitutes that have been proposed, for accent and inflection are by no means always coincident. I have not always been careful to distinguish between *metre* and *rhythm,* and I have used *line* and *verse* as synonyms, for it seems too late to struggle against the confusion into which these terms have fallen: and when convenience suggested it, I have not scrupled to speak of *feet* and *inversions* of feet, even in cases where I should be most reluctant to admit the scientific accuracy of the terms.

Finally, in the matter of orthography in the Latin and French extracts, I have generally followed without comment the editions from which I actually transcribed (as March and Bartsch); and I have not noted *variae lectiones,* which are of course numerous, except where they affected some question directly in issue.

New Haven, September 1897.

C. M. L.

TABLE OF CONTENTS.

CHAPTER I. Introduction.

		Page
§ 1.	The principle of parallelism	1
§ 2.	Syllabic verse	2
§ 3.	Quantitative verse	3
§ 4.	Accentual verse	4
§ 5.	The decay of Greek versification	4
§ 6.	Origin and decay of Latin quantitative versification	6
§ 7.	The problems of late Latin verse	8
§ 8.	The theory of a popular origin (for the Latin "rhythms")	9
§ 9.	Popular verse of irregular rhythm (not syllabic)	9
§ 10.	Conclusion	12

CHAPTER II. Commodian's verse.

§ 11.	The importance of the subject	13
§ 12.	Meyer's theory	14
§ 13.	Objections to Meyer's theory	16
§ 14.	Commodian's use of dissyllables	16
§ 15.	Commodian's use of polysyllables	18
§ 16.	The rationale of Commodian's verse	20
§ 17.	Commodian's treatment of the cæsura	21
§ 18.	Concluding remarks	22

CHAPTER III. The Latin Hymns of Ambrose and his Followers.

§ 19.	Introductory remarks	24
§ 20.	Ambrose	25
§ 21.	Sedulius	26
§ 22.	Fortunatus	28
§ 23.	Substitution of accent for prosodical length	30
§ 24.	Early hymns of uncertain date	31
§ 25.	Ambrosian hymns of Adam of St. Victor	32
§ 26.	Trochaics of Adam of St. Victor	35
§ 27.	The invention of the initial inversion	39

CHAPTER IV. Early Church Music: Syllabic Verse.

§ 28.	Introduction	43
§ 29.	Greek music	44
§ 30.	The music of Ambrose	45
§ 31.	Music of the Roman Empire in general	47
§ 32.	St. Augustine's psalm	48
§ 33.	The music of Augustine's psalm	50
§ 34.	The two schools of church music	52
§ 35.	The influence of the church music on versification	54
§ 36.	Contemporary accounts of the Latin rhythms	57
§ 37.	Conclusion	57

CHAPTER V. Early French Verse.

§ 38.	Introduction	63
§ 39.	Modern French verse	64
§ 40.	The origin of French versification	68
§ 41.	The earliest French octosyllabics	70
§ 42.	The later development of French octosyllabics	73
§ 43.	The difference between Latin and Old French verse	75
§ 44.	Explanation of the difference	77
§ 45.	Explanation of the change in French verse	83
§ 46.	French Decasyllabics	87

CHAPTER VI. Latin and French Influence in English verse.

§ 47.	Old English verse	91
§ 48.	The decay of Old English verse	92
§ 49.	Development of English verse under foreign influence	94
§ 50.	Chaucer	97
§ 51.	The syllabic principle in Modern English verse	99

BIBLIOGRAPHY

of the principal authorities referred to in the notes.

AMBROS, A. W. Geschichte der Musik, mit zahlreichen Notenbeispielen und Musikbeilagen. (Vol. II, 2nd ed.). Leipzig 1880.

BARTSCH, KARL. Chrestomathie de L'Ancien Français (VIIIe— XVe Siècles), accompagnée d'une Grammaire et d'un Glossaire. Cinquième éd., corrigée et augmentée, Leipzig, 1884.

BRIDGES, ROBERT. Milton's Prosody, an Examination of the Rules of Blank Verse in Milton's later poems. * * * * Oxford, 1893.

CHAPPEL, WILLIAM. The History of Music (Art and Science). Vol. I, from the earliest records to the fall of the Roman Empire. London, 1874.

DU MÉRIL, E. I. Poésies populaires latines antérieures au douzième siècle. Paris, 1843.

—— II. Poésies populaires latines du moyen age. Paris, 1847.

FÉTIS, F. J. Histoire générale de la musique depuis les temps les plus anciens jusqu'à nos jours. Paris, 1869—76.

—— Biogràphie universelle des Musiciens et bibliographie générale de la musique. 2e éd. Paris, 1873.

GAUTIER, LÉON. Les Épopées Françaises. Étude sur les origines et l'histoire de la littérature nationale. 2e éd. Paris, 1878 à 1882.

JULIAN, JOHN. A Dictionary of Hymnology, setting forth the origin and history of Christian Hymns of all ages and nations, * * *. London, 1892.

KAWCZYNSKI, MAXIMILIEN. Essai comparatif sur L'Origine et L'Histoire des Rhythmes. Paris, 1889.

LUBARSCH, E. Französische Verslehre * * *. Berlin, 1879.

MARCH, F. A. Latin Hymns, with English Notes. For use in schools and colleges. New York, 1874.

MAYOR, T. B. Chapters on English Metre. Cambridge, 1886.

MEYER, WILHELM. Anfang und Ursprung der lateinischen und griechischen rythmischen Dichtung. Munich, 1884.

MONRO, D. B. The Modes of Ancient Greek Music. Oxf., 1894.
PARIS, GASTON. Étude sur le rôle de l'accent latin dans la langue française. Paris, 1862.
—— Lettre à Léon Gautier sur la versification latine rhythmique. Paris, 1866.
SCHIPPER, J. Englische Metrik, in historischer und systematischer Entwickelung dargestellt. Erster Theil Altenglische Metrik, Bonn, 1881.
SIEVERS, G. E. Altgermanische Metrik. Halle, 1893.
STENGEL, EDMUND. Romanische Verslehre (in Gröber's Grundriss der Romanischen Philologie, II. Bd., 1. Abt., 1. Liefg.). Strassburg, 1893.
WESTPHAL, RUDOLF (and HUGO GLEDITSCH). Allgemeine Theorie der Griechischen Metrik, (being the 3rd vol. of Die Theorie der musischen Künste der Hellenen, by ROSSBACH and WESTPHAL). Leipzig, 1887.

CHAPTER I.
Introduction.

§ 1. *The principle of parallelism.* The simplest known form of civilized verse is that of the Hebrew scriptures. In the poetical parts of the Bible there is present no regular principle of versification except that of the correspondence (or, more technically, parallelism) of one clause with another. This form is probably not only the simplest but the oldest known:—indeed according to Old Testament chronology it is not long antedated by the creation, for it is found in the song of Lamech to his wives.

> Hear my voice;
> Ye wives of Lamech hearken unto my speech:
>
> For I have slain a man to my wounding,
> And a young man to my hurt.
>
> If Cain shall be avenged sevenfold,
> Truly Lamech seventy and sevenfold.(1)

This principle of parallelism is of course present in all the more modern forms of verse: it is indeed fundamental in the theory of æsthetics. From it, probably, are developed all other forms. We have, however, no

---

(1) Gen. IV, 23. The parallelism is sometimes more or less complicated; and in some of the Psalms the use of a recurring refrain seems to indicate a strophic arrangement. Efforts have been made to work out a strict metrical scheme for some of the Hebrew poems, but they have not won much favor.

modern poetry of any great importance in which this principle is the only determinant of form: our modern systems of verse differ among themselves in respect to the various refinements to which this principle has been subjected, but it appears in them all only as a theoretical base.

§ 2. *Syllabic verse.* Probably the first important advance from this crude stage of art is to be seen in the syllabic verse of some of the oldest parts of the Avesta. Here the principle of parallelism is still seen in comparative undress, but the parallel periods are all composed of equal numbers of syllables. The effect may be shown (for those who, like the present writer, have no knowledge of the original) in an English reproduction of the verse-form.(1)

Who was the first of all mortals | to honor thee on earth, Homa?
What reward was bestowed on him,| what honor conferred upon him?
Vivaswan was the first mortal | to do me honor upon Earth;
He therefore was so rewarded, | such honor was conferred on him,
That he had a son born to him, | the all-powerful King Jima,
The most worshipful of mortals, | the deliverer of mankind.

Each verse contains 16 syllables, distinctly divided into hemistichs of 8 syllables each. So far as has yet been proved, there is no regular recurrence of long and short, or of stressed and unstressed syllables. In other words, the verse is what we will call purely syllabic. A curious specimen of a similar form of verse is found in a Latin MS. of the 9th century, in a poem on the removal of a Saint's relics.(2)

---

(1) From a German translation from the first part of the *Yasna*, given by Westphal, p. 41. The German translation is in modern accentual rhythm: 'Wer hat als der Menschen erster dich verehrt auf Erden, Homa?' I have obliterated the rhythm, for the sake of conforming to Westphal's own description,—upon which that in the text is founded.

(2) Given by Du Méril I, 162, as from Massmann, *Die deutschen Abschwörungs-, Glaubens-, Beicht- und Bet-Formeln*, p. 8 n. 17.

Beatissimus namque Dionysius | Athenis quondam episcopus,
Quem Sanctus Clemens direxit in Galliam | propter praedicandi
[gratiam,
Ibidemque martyrio coronatus | comperitur, et tumulatus, etc.

Each verse contains 21 syllables, with a cæsura after the 12th. No further regularity, either metrical or rhythmical, can be perceived. Such a verse could probably not have been written except for music, but the specimen is given here because it is one of the very few available in which the syllabic principle appears *alone*.(1) In combination with other principles, we shall find it of great importance, in English as well as in Latin and French.

§ 3. *Quantitative verse.* The second in order of the more modern kinds of verse is that which depends upon the quantity of syllables. Quantitative verse is thought, with much reason, to have developed out of the purely syllabic form.(2) Thus the octosyllabic hemistich of the form

$$\times \times \times \times \times \times \times \times$$

(where $\times$ represents a syllable of indeterminate quantity) was in time supplanted by one of the form

$$\times \times \times \times \times - \smile -.$$

The verse-end has often proved itself peculiarly sensitive, and liable to change; and if such a change as this could once get a firm hold on the verse-end, it is easy to see how it might quickly extend itself to the whole verse. This is hardly more, however, than speculation, and we must for the present accept the appearance of quantitative verse, in (for example) the earliest known Greek poetry, as one of our ultimate facts. It may have developed from a prehistoric Aryan verse, in which only the syllabic principle was recognized, or it may possibly have been an original creation of the Hellenic race. Its characteristic forms are too familiar to need description here.

---

(1) I. e. without the aid even of rime, in the modern sense.
(2) Westphal, p. 45.

§ 4. *Accentual verse.* The third and last of the distinct principles of modern verse-structure is that which regulates the verse according to word-accent. This is commonly recognized as the controlling principle of English verse, but it is now generally to be found only in combination with the syllabic principle, or at least marked and defined by end-rime. It is worth noting, however, that in Old English verse this principle relied for its external support upon quantity and alliteration, and that these two, as essential principles of English verse, have passed away as rime and syllabism came in. The accentual principle may therefore be regarded as the sole native base of our modern system of verse, even though it is so seldom to be observed in its native state. So far as the writer is aware, it has never held sole sway in any prevailing form of verse, though isolated examples may be given. Thus in Old and Middle English poetry there are occasional lines in which we find neither alliteration nor rime nor regard for quantity; but they are exceptions, not types. Perhaps the best specimen of purely accentual verse that can be given is Charles Lamb's "*The Old Familiar Faces*":

> I have had playmates, I have had companions,
> In my days of childhood, in my joyful school-days;
> All, all are gone, the old familiar faces.

§ 5. *The decay of Greek versification.* However uncertain the origin of quantitative Greek verse, we can be sure that it had its justification in the nature of the spoken language. The Greeks wrote in quantity because they spoke in quantity, just as the modern English poet writes what we call accentual verse because his language is in the main an accentual language. On the other hand it is clear that the quantitative system of Greek poetry was in part artificial. It seems impossible that every long syllable should require in ordinary speech just twice the time of any short syllable; and some of the phenomena of logaoedic measures are obviously due to arbitrary conventions. In post-classical times, the relations between quantity in speech and quantity in verse seem gradually to have become still more strained. For example the rhetorician Dionysius of Halicarnassus, writing in the first century B. C., says of the famous Homeric line on Sisyphus: "its most striking peculiarity is this:—neither of the long feet which are apt to be found in heroic verse, (i. e. spondees or bacchii), occurs here except in the last place: the first five feet are all dactyls, and that too of the sort that have their second syllables slurred over; so that some of them are not very different from trochees".(1) In other words, some of the short syllables in αὖθις ἔπειτα πέδονδε, &c., were markedly shorter than others, in the time of Dionysius if not before. Moreover the character of the Greek accent was also changing. From a mere inflection (as it seems to have been in the time of Aristoxenus,(2)) it had become in the time of Babrius a marked stress.(3) Quantitative verse had been made easy by the quantitative character of the language and by an almost entire absence of accentual stress:—but as the former decayed and the latter came in, quantitative writing became more and more an act of somewhat pedantic affectation; and

---

(1) Ὁ δὲ μάλιστα τῶν ἄλλων θαυμάζειν ἄξιον, ῥυθμὸς οὐδεὶς τῶν μακρῶν, οἳ Φύσιν ἔχουσι πίπτειν εἰς μέτρον ἡρῷον, οὔτε σπονδεῖος οὔτε βακχεῖος, ἐγκαταμέμικται τῷ στίχῳ πλὴν ἐπὶ τῆς τελευτῆς. οἱ δὲ ἄλλοι πάντες εἰσὶ δάκτυλοι καὶ οὗτοί γε παραδεδιωγμένας ἔχοντες τὰς ἀλόγους, ὥστε μὴ πολὺ διαφέρειν ἐνίους τῶν τροχαίων. (De Comp. Verb. c. 20, cited by Westphal, p. 16). The meaning of ἀλόγους, as Westphal points out, is not clear, as the word is ordinarily applied only to naturally long syllables that are irrationally slurred. Obviously, however, it here designates the second syllable of the foot, and it presumably indicates that Homer's dactyls were understood by Dionysius as cyclic.

(2) See, for example Marquardt's ed. of *Arist. Fragm.*, p. 24, l. 15.

(3) As is shown by B.'s peculiar treatment of the Choliambic.

the poets had to meet the new conditions of the language by writing a new kind of verse.(1)

§ 6. *Origin and decay of Latin quantitative versification.* The later developments in Latin literature were similar, but the beginning seems to have been different. That the earliest known forms of Latin verse were of an accentual character seems now fairly established.(2) The quantitative system was not a spontaneous creation of the Romans, nor apparently the natural outcome of any peculiar fashion in their mode of speech, but was an exotic, engrafted upon their literature in the 3rd century B. C. by students of Greek. It could not have thriven at Rome if the Latin language had not been more markedly quantitative (and perhaps less accentual) than, for example, modern English: but it would hardly have been necessary to go abroad for it if the language had not been naturally less prone to it than the Greek.(3) That the application of the Greek system to the Latin tongue must have involved something of a wrench is clear enough,(4) and there is reason for believing that accentual poetry, even through the classical age, kept a place in the ear of the common people. Apparent

---

(1) In the following pages I shall not develop this branch of the subject, because, although the Greek and Latin literatures were so related that a mutual influence in the matter of versification seems very probable *a priori*, yet in fact the progress in Latin verse seems self-explanatory. It is only with the latter that we are directly concerned, and I have observed no decisive evidence that the Greek verse is even indirectly relevant, except as presenting an interesting parallel.

(2) Lindsay, *Am. Journal of Phil.*, Vol. 14 (1893), p. 139.

(3) Kawczynski says, (p. 30), "les influences historiques sont plus fortes que les conditions naturelles", and the phenomena of classical Latin metres seem to support his assertion. I think we shall find, however, that this is an isolated case. At all events, the generalization is unwarranted.

(4) Cf. the artificial way in which the Roman poets treated the complexities of logaoedic verse.

remnants of it are found, for example, in the song of Aurelian's soldiers,

Tantum vini habet nemo quantum fudit sanguinis,

and the song of the 6th legion,

Mille Francos, mille semel Sarmatas occidimus.(1)

It seems not impossible that a keen ear for prosody,—a nice perception of quantities,—may have been something of a rarity even among the upper classes in the Augustan age. But assuming that it was lacking then only among the uncultivated, it is certain that in the succeeding centuries the educated classes lost it too. As early as the beginning of the 5th century the difference between long and short syllables was no more practical to the average Roman than it is now to the average Englishman. This is shown by a curious passage in St. Augustine's treatise on music. The treatise is in the form of an imaginary conversation between teacher and pupil. At one point the teacher purposely misquotes Virgil's line

Arma virumque cano, Trojae qui *primis* ab oris.

And the student is unable to see that the excellence of the verse is in any way impaired.(2) And the grammarian Servius, writing probably at about the same time, says most explicitly:—"Quod pertinat ad naturam primae syllabae, longane sit aut brevis, solis confirmamus exemplis; medias vero in latino sermone accentu discernimus; ultimas arte colligimus."(3) In other words even the most highly educated Romans learned the quantity of penults only from the accent, and that of other syllables only from the example of the poets or from established rules. Usage in pronunciation was no guide.

Under these circumstances, the composition of quantitative poetry began in Latin as in Greek to involve too

---

(1) Cf. also Horace, Ep. II. 1. 157: "*Hodieque manent* vestigia ruris".

(2) *De Musica*, II. 2.

(3) *De Ratione Ultimarum Syllabarum*, as quoted by G. Paris, *Sur l'accent lat.* p. 30, n. 2.

much of pedantry: and as in Greece during the Byzantine period, so in Rome during the dark ages, the art of writing syllabic or accentual verse grew gradually in favour, until the old style had been effectually ousted from the field of lyric poetry. In the Romance languages, then in process of formation, one of the new styles was adopted for all kinds of poetry, to the entire exclusion of the old.

§ 7. *The problems of late Latin verse.* The object of the first part of this paper will be to trace and explain. so far as possible, the processes of decay just mentioned, The problem may be provisionally divided into two parts, In the first place, was the late Latin verse essentially accentual, or was it merely syllabic? In the second place. how did the poets acquire the new art? The answer to the first question most favored by contemporary scholarship (notably by Wilhelm Meyer) is in substance that the so-called "rhythmical" form of the late Latin hymns was not based upon accent at all; that as quantitative verse passed into "rhythmical", the element that survived was not the true rhythm of metrical stress, but merely the parallelism that was enforced by uniformity in the number of syllables per verse; and that when there seems to be a strictly accentual rhythm in the later verses, its appearance is in general the result of a happy chance, not at any rate an essential condition of the verse.

To the second question the answers have been various, but we may group the most important of them under three heads. The later "rhythmical" system, according to modern opinion, was derived either (1) from the quantitative system by a natural transition, not the result of external influences, or (2) from foreign sources, either as an entire importation or (according to Meyer) as a sort of graft upon the decayed quantitative system, or (3) from the popular accentual verse of the earlier days of Rome.

§ 8. *The theory of a popular origin.* The last theory deserves some attention, although its strongest advocate has withdrawn his support.(1) It has been contended that there existed a continuous literature (if it deserves the name) of accentual poetry, from the earliest to the latest age of the Latin language, beginning with the Saturnian verse, manifesting itself in the classical epoch in the popular songs of which specimens have already been given, and culminating in the triumph of the accentual system.

It is unnecessary to repeat the arguments that have been advanced against this contention,(2) but, if it should still be regarded as plausible, it is worth while to point out that it does not explain the phenomena that most need explanation in our present study. All the fragments of popular song that have been cited in support of this theory are in a trochaic rhythm. The two verses already quoted in these pages are fairly representative. Now (as will be shown hereafter) the trochaic rhythm was of no direct influence in the development of those Romance verse-forms to which the great body of English verse is indebted. We may fancy that we see in the song of Aurelian's soldiers the direct progenitor of such poems as the anonymous "*De Gaudiis Paradisi*":—

> Ad perennis vitae fontem mens sitivit arida,
> Claustra carnis praesto frangi clausa quaerit anima,
> Gliscit, ambit, eluctatur exul, frui patria.

But we should search French literature in vain for any verse imitated from the latter.

§ 9. *Popular verse of irregular rhythm.* There are however certain other evidences which may tend to show

---

(1) G. PARIS. Compare his *Lettre à M. Léon Gautier*, with his note in *Romania* XV. 138.

(2) They are well reviewed by MEYER, pp. 107—8;—although, as will appear in the next chapter, the argument based on Commodian's experiments is easily refutable.

the continuous existence of a popular Latin versification of an accentual character. The popular songs already mentioned were perhaps merely sporadic,—ignorant imitations of a form of quantitative verse heard at the Roman theatres. Those which we are now to consider, on the other hand, seem to have no connection with any quantitative verse. There is preserved from the 7th century a collection of curious letters that passed between Bishop Frodebertus and a person styled Importunus. They are written in a sort of hap-hazard accentual rhythm, not much better than their latinity, as an example will show:

> Amas puella bella
> De qualibet terra,
> Pro nulla bonitate
> Nec sancta caritate.
> Bonus nunquam eris,
> Dum tale via tenes.
> Per tua cauta longa,
> Satis est, vel non est?(1)

This is not much better than prose, and it really seems unnecessary to believe that the author had ever seen any rhythm of the kind before:—to have invented it out of whole cloth would have required no great effort of ingenuity. But there are those(2) who have little belief in any natural *penchant* of ignorant men for rhythmical expression, and seek more or less confidently for precedents for all such phenomena. It is certainly not impossible that Frodebertus and Importunus may belong to an undiscovered order of popular Latin versifiers, with an unbroken file of predecessors reaching back to the earliest times: their verse certainly resembles the Saturnian as closely as does that of the soldiers' songs. In that

---

(1) BOUCHERIE, *Cinq Formules Rhythmées et Assonancées du VII. Siècle*, (Montpellier 1867), p. 26.

(2) Notably Kawczynski. See *ante*, § 6, note, and his "*Essai*", *passim*.

case, the following rhythmical invitation to dinner, from a 10th century MS.(1) may belong to the same family of verse.

> Jam dulcis amica venito
> Quam sicut cor meum diligo;
> Intra in cubiculum meum,
> Ornamentis cunctis onustum.
> Ibi sunt sedilia strata
> Et domus velis ornata, etc.

It should be remarked however, that these verses, like the trochaic songs before mentioned, are not paralleled by the ordinary forms of French verse. A striking peculiarity of the Latin lines just quoted is that in them the number of syllables per verse is altogether irregular.(2) It happens, to be sure, that the earliest extant specimen of French verse, the song in honor of St. Eulalia, is indeed written in a rhythm which at first glance seems vaguely similar to that employed by Importunus:—

> Buona pulcella fut Eulalia
> Bel avret corps, bellezour anima.
> Voldrent la veintre li Deo inimi,
> Voldrent la faire diavle servir.
> Elle non eskoltet les mals conseillers,
> Qu'elle Deo raneiet chi maent sus en ciel, etc.

But the Eulalia verse is known to be of very different origin;(3)—and it is, moreover, unique in early French literature.(4) However numerous, therefore, compositions

---

(1) Given by Du Méril, II. 196.

(2) In the "Invitation" it varies from 8 to 10: in the letters it varies still more widely.

(3) It is clearly modeled upon a Latin sequence.

(4) Unless we possibly should class it with such defective verses as those in the *Enseignements Salomon* and certain Anglo-Norman poems, which require to be scanned by the number of accents rather than syllables. Of these, however, the former, if not corrupt, are doubtless simply bad verses; and the latter are due to the retro-active influence of English verse. Even these Anglo-Norman verses are regarded by STENGEL as merely unskilled work, for as he points out, (p. 11), GOWER and Frère ANGER wrote correctly. In any case, to connect them with the Eulalia would be quite wild.

of this character may have been in the dark ages, they left no permanent traces in later literatures. The only verses, whether Latin or French, which concern the present inquiry, are those in which the syllabic principle is maintained,—either with or without an accentual rhythm.

§ 10. *Conclusion.* It is clear therefore that the controlling influences for which we are searching are not to be found in Latin popular poetry.(1) The other branches of the problem will require more extended discussion. The chapters immediately succeeding will state certain reasons for believing that the later "rhythms" grew out of quantitative verse by a gradual and natural process; and in the course of the investigation an effort will be made to show that the somewhat old-fashioned belief that these "rhythms" were really rhythmical (i. e. accentual), has been too hastily discarded. If Meyer's theory of the nature of the late Latin verse is the wrong one, then his theory as to its origin need not detain us long, for the two are inter-dependent.

---

(1) Stengel's and Blanc's theory of a lost popular Latin rhythm, the parent of the French 10-syllable verse, may be disregarded:—for as will appear hereafter, that verse is not in the direct line of descent from Latin to English. The specimens of irregular verse that have just been cited are doubtless mere slovenly imitations of the regular rhythms to be examined later.

CHAPTER II.
Commodian's Verse.

§ 11. *The importance of the subject.* One of the most important questions to be determined is whether, as the Roman poets lost their ear for quantity, the feeling which remained uppermost was the feeling for rhythmical run and stress, or only the feeling for parallelism and uniformity in the counting of syllables. This is indeed but another way of stating the main question at issue, for if the rhythmical ictus survived, then the later versification would of course be accentual as well as syllabic:— otherwise it would be syllabic but not accentual. It has been ably urged that whatever there may have been in the nature of ictus, in the classical quantitative verse, it was not separable from the quantitative system, but perished with it:—and strong confirmation of this belief has been found in the apparently unrhythmical character of the verse of Commodian, a writer of the transition period. This poet, about the middle of the 3rd century of our era, introduced the practice of writing hexameters of a barbarous kind, which not only were not strictly quantitative, but also seemingly failed to attain any smoothness of accentual rhythm. His so-called *"Carmen Apologeticum"*, a poem of some 1060 lines, begins as follows:—

> Quis poterit unum proprie Deum nosse coelorum,
> Nisi quem is tulerit [longe] ab errore nefando?

Errabam ignarus spatians, spe captus inani,(1)
Dum furor aetatis primae me portabat in auras.
Plus eram quam palea levior: quasi centum inessent
In umeris capita, sic praeceps quocumque ferebar.

The question for us to determine is whether these lines were meant to be read and scanned like quantitative hexameters, thus:

Quis pote | rit u | num ‖ propri | e Deum | nosse coe | lorum
Nisi quem | is tule | rit ‖ lon | ge ab er | rore ne | fando :(2)

or whether (as Meyer contends) they should be read with their natural prose accents. A definite solution of the problem will go far toward establishing the true theory of the later "rhythms".

§ 12. *Meyer's theory.* The prose-accent theory seems at first glance particularly plausible. Commodian cannot have written in ignorance of the true nature of the hexameter, or of the laws of quantity, for in certain respects (as will be pointed out hereafter) he observes those laws with care: he was, moreover, a man of wide reading, and it is not easy to see how such a man could scan his lines in the excruciating manner indicated above. The probability is(3) that Commodian deliberately rejected what had already become a highly artificial mode of composition, because he thought it unsuitable for the expression of Christian earnestness:—and having rejected it in part, one might expect him to reject the artificial elements of it altogether.

Meyer's contention is ably reasoned, and the present writer can add nothing to this side of the argument except a suggestion as to the practical effect which

---

(1) This is indeed a good hexameter, and so are several others of Commodian's lines: —they are so however, only by accident. In this case the accident is obvious, for the line was certainly designed to be read without elision.

(2) Cf. Tennyson's burlesque: "These lame hexameters the strong-winged music of Homer"; —and the Elizabethan hexameters generally.

(3) This suggestion was first made, I think, by Du Méril.

Commodian may have designed. Meyer says (p. 302) "Demnach findet sich bei Commodian nur die eine Rücksicht auf den Wortaccent, dass er, wie die quantitirenden Dichter, in die fünfte Hebung stets eine Silbe rückte, welche den Wortaccent hatte, während es ihm nahe lag, das nicht zu thun. Dies ist der einzige Fall, von dem man sagen darf, dass Commodian sich um den Wortaccent mehr gekümmert habe als Virgil oder Ovid": Here Meyer seems to weaken his own case by representing the structure of these verses as comparatively purposeless. If Commodian designed his lines to be read according to their prose accents, there can be no doubt that he was consciously imitating the effect produced by such a reading of strictly quantitative hexameters, and that he wished his lines to sound to his unlearned contemporaries substantially as Virgil's or Ovid's must have sounded. Such a verse, for example, as Commodian's
    Sub jugo servili ut portent victalia collo   (Inst. 39, 16).
fairly reproduces the accentual rhythm of Virgil's
    Aut age diversos, et disice corpora ponto.   (Aen. I, 70.)
To match every verse of Commodian's with a verse from Virgil would be a forbidding task, owing to the great variety of possible combinations; but if the verses are split into hemistichs the latter can be matched without difficulty. Thus the following hemistichs from Virgil will be found to tally with the passage cited above from the *Carmen Apologeticum.*

Hinc populum late (21)(1)	Latio genus unde Latinum (6)
Ipsa Jovis rapidum (42)	Stridens Aquilone procella (102)
Italiam fato (2)	Meritis pro talibus annos (74)
Et soror et conjunx (47)	Memorem Junonis ob iram (4)
Judicium Paridis (27)	Animam hanc effundere dextra (98)
Andierat Tyrias (20)	O terque quaterque beati (94).

(1) The numbers refer to lines in the 1st Book of the Aeneid. I may add that from the same book I found no difficulty in matching each hemistich in the 39th of the *Instructiones* (containing 26 lines), having selected that passage quite at random.

§ 13. *Objections to Meyer's theory*. But plausible as is this theory about Commodian's verse-structure, there is an insuperable objection to it; and the substance of that objection is, in part, so carefully stated by Meyer himself, that it is hard to see how he failed to appreciate its weight. The fact is that in certain respects Commodian is strictly attentive to quantity, and it seems almost perverse to accept any theory which reduces this laborious strictness to "todter Zierrat". Meyer himself points out (p. 291) that of the 490 verses of the *Carmen Apol.* which end with dissyllables, there are only two in which the penultimate syllable is short; also (p. 296) that the penultimate syllable of the first hemistich is always strictly correct in quantity. The significance of the first of these facts is perhaps not obvious at first sight. It will be observed, however, that when the verse ended with a polysyllable, the penultimate syllable would necessarily be long, for otherwise the desired accentual effect would fail; but in the poet's use of dissyllables one would expect to find him utterly capricious as to quantity, since in such words the accent is necessarily on the penult. Here then Meyer finds indisputable proof not only that Commodian understood quantity but that at the end of each hemistich he was careful to observe it. On page 296 he says "Die Bildung des Schlusses war Commodian die Hauptsache"; in the remaining parts of each verse he finds (with a few exceptions which need not be noted here) nothing but entire indifference.

§ 14. *Commodian's use of dissyllables*. But as a matter of fact it can be shown that Commodian's regard for quantity extended much further than even Meyer has observed. The latter's remark upon dissyllables at the ends of verses naturally suggests an inquiry into the use of dissyllables elsewhere; and it will be found that the quantity of their penults is observed as carefully in all parts of the verse as it is at the end. This observance of quantity follows a very curious but simple law. If the verses are read rhythmically, (i. e. with the same rhythmical movement as that of quantitative hexameters), it will be found that the thesis generally falls on the first syllable of a dissyllabic word *only if that syllable is really long*:—if, on the other hand, the first syllable of such a word stands in the arsis, then that syllable if long may form part of either a dactyl or a spondee, but if short can form part only of a dactyl.

This law can easily be demonstrated by an analysis of a passage from one of Commodian's poems. For example, in the first hundred lines of the *Carmen Apologeticum* there are some 108(1) dissyllables of which the penults will receive the thesis if the verses are read as quantitative hexameters. Of these, 52 are at the ends of lines, constituting in each case, of course, the 6th foot of the line. Of the latter all but two (edunt, l. 22, and quoque,(2) l. 41) have the first syllable long. Of the other 56, which are found in the first, second, fourth and fifth feet of the lines,(3) all but three have the first syllable long, the exceptions being nisi (2), datas (27) and bonum (87).(4) This almost perfect regularity is not due to any overwhelming preponderance of trochaic or spondaic dissyllables in the Latin language, for there is no such preponderance:—and it is not due to any whimsical avoidance by Commodian of dissyllables with short penults; for in this same passage such dissyllables occur to the number of 59, and all except the three just mentioned stand with their penults in the arsis. Furthermore,—and this is perhaps the most curious fact to be observed,— of all the 56 dissyllables with short penults standing in

---

(1) This is without deduction for repetitions.
(2) Which Meyer seems to have overlooked.
(3) Not in the third, for Commodian puts his cæsura there.
(4) Perhaps also prius (83) should be added, making a total of 4 out of 57: —but I am doubtful as to the scansion of this line.

the arsis, only one is so placed that its penult forms part of a spondee. This single exception is statim (12). In all the other cases the penults stand properly for the short syllables of metrical dactyls. If, on the other hand, the penult of a dissyllable is long, then it may be in the thesis or the arsis indifferently, and in the latter case may be treated as either long or short. No system seems to prevail here, except at the close of the first hemistich (as will be pointed out hereafter). Compare for example the hemistich

                Et lumen offerimus (76)
or   Si pinguis est opibus (23)
with   Et nemo scibat (46).

§ 15. *Commodian's use of polysyllables.* This curious system in the use of dissyllables seems quite inexplicable, unless the rhythmical reading of the verses (which we have assumed) was that really designed by Commodian. If that was really the case, it seems a fair working hypothesis (first) that Commodian was writing verse in quantity, so far as quantity was perceptible in his generation, in ordinary speech and to unscholarly ears, and (second) that for some reason the quantity of accented syllables was more marked and determinate than that of syllables not accented. If this were the case, then the same system would probably prevail in the use of polysyllables;—and an examination will show that in fact it does.

In the first hundred lines of the *Carmen Apologeticum* Commodian uses some 255 polysyllabic words. The accented syllables of these words are long in 182 cases, short in 73. Of these 182 long syllables, 140 stand in the thesis, 42 in the arsis. Of these 42 again, 17 are found in spondees and 25 in dactyls. A majority, therefore, of those that stand in the arsis, are improperly used. Of the 73 short syllables, on the other hand, 67 are used in the unstressed parts of dactyls, while *none* occur in the unstressed parts of spondees, and only 6 receive the metrical thesis. These 6 exceptions are found in *divitiis* (20) and *divitias* (27), *humiles* (29) and *humilem* (92), *praeposuit* (35), and *arbitrio* (85): and they practically reduce to three, for two of them are repetitions, and in *arbitrio* the penult may well have been regarded as long by position. It is worth noting, also, that in each of these exceptional cases the irregular foot is a dactyl, not a spondee;—and that the same is true where a dissyllable is irregularly used. Thus in the second line of the passage quoted above, the irregular foot is *nisi quem*, not *nisi* alone. Apparently the presence of two other syllables in the foot made it easier to tolerate the impropriety:—or perhaps, indeed, we should say that Commodian did not regard these feet as dactyls at all, but that he sometimes allowed himself the license of substituting a tribrach. Such a substitution was of course not authorized by precedent: but it was logical and natural enough when all the dactyls were understood as cyclic, and of course Commodian cared little for precedent.

There is yet a further peculiarity in Commodian's use of polysyllables which remains to be noted. Where the accent, in Latin, is proparoxytone, the penult is of course always short. In the hundred lines now under examination these penults are *never* misused. In other words, not one of them receives the thesis, or stands in the arsis of a spondee. This uniform recognition of the quantity of short penults is sufficient to account for one of the facts stated in the last paragraph, namely the absence of short accented antepenultimate syllables from spondaic feet: for if such a syllable could finish a spondee, then a short penult would have to begin the next foot:— but the statement was made as it stands for the sake of completeness, and because, moreover, the appearance of the same phenomenon in dissyllables shows that it would doubtless appear in polysyllables also as an independent fact, without this special necessity.

§ 16. *The rationale of Commodian's verse.* As to Commodian's treatment of the quantity of syllables in general it remains only to say that in monosyllables, and in all parts of other words except accented syllables and short penults, he shows entire indifference.(1) But that his practice in the matter of accented antepenults and short penults should be merely fortuitous, or anything but deliberate and systematic, is impossible. Moreover it is obvious that this practice must be capable of explanation and justification by the phenomena of ordinary speech in Commodian's time. To give such an explanation with thoroughness and certainty, is beyond the scope of this paper and beyond the writer's present ability; but the evidence seems irresistible that Commodian was writing in prosody as it existed in his own day. The common speech of his contemporaries seems to have exhibited a phase of transition between that of Virgil and that of St. Augustine's pupil. The quantity of accented syllables seems to have been appreciated by the unaided ear.(2) If they were long they could be slurred, but if they were short the poet was careful to avoid drawling them. Of syllables which did not bear the accent no particular account was taken, for their quantity, if perceptible, was at any rate not boldly marked. Perhaps only scholars knew whether they were long or short. If so, the use of these syllables by the classical poets must have seemed purely capricious to the unscholarly, and therefore Commodian might properly use them as convenience dictated.(3)

---

(1) Except, of course, in the special cases mentioned in the next section.

(2) Of this exceptional definiteness in the pronunciation of accented syllables there is perhaps a remnant in the law of the preservation of the accented syllables in the passage from Low Latin into French.

(3) Of course his treatment of unaccented penults needs no explanation. Such syllables were known to be short by the rules of accent, whether they were so pronounced or not.

§ 17. *Commodian's treatment of the Cæsura.* There is yet one other peculiarity in these verses of Commodian's. He observes the strict rules of quantity in one set of cases, (namely in the penultimate syllable of each first hemistich), which cannot be explained as dependent upon the accents of the words at all. Meyer says (p. 296): "Die Bildung des Schlusses war Commodian die Hauptsache. Die letzte Silbe der beiden Halbzeilen, in welche er die Langzeile des Hexameters zerlegt,(1) ist von ihm als Zeilenschluss behandelt und frei gegeben". [Perhaps we should say, its quantity is indifferent because it is the final syllable *of a word*:—thus in l. 6 of the specimen given above, *capita* receives the same treatment as *poterit* in l. 1]. "Dagegen ist ihm die Bildung der vorletzten Silbe die Hauptsache. Diese ist so gut wie immer quantitirend recht gebildet". Here Meyer is undoubtedly right. In many cases, to be sure, the penultimate syllable of the first hemistich must be correct in quantity, by the rules already discovered: thus if the cæsura is preceded by a polysyllable or dissyllable whose penult is short, then the second foot of the line must be a dactyl, and the quantity of the syllable in question is exactly what it should be. But there are other cases which can be explained only upon Meyer's principle. Thus, for example, in the first hundred lines of the *Carmen Apologeticum*, the first hemistich is six times ended with a monosyllable, e. g.

Spero reus non est (81):
Interdum quod meum est (83):—

and in every case the syllable preceding, though final, is correct in quantity.

Two explanations of this are possible, first that this attentiveness to quantity at the cæsura was merely a bit of pedantic affectation, or second that the quantity

---

(1) Note again that the cæsura is always penthemimeral.

even of final syllables was still barely distinguishable in Commodian's time, and that therefore while it could be disregarded elsewhere, it must be heeded in those parts of the line in which grace was most needed. The latter supposition seems more plausible.

§ 18. *Concluding remarks.* Further support for the opinion that Commodian's system was closely related to his mode of speech, may be found in the pseudo-hexametrical poems of the 8th century;(1) for although they were seemingly made in imitation of Commodian's verse, they do not exhibit the chief peculiarities of his system at all. Thus in the *Exhortatio Poenitendi* we find such lines as

>Mens confusa taediis itinera devia carpens (3)
>Nec casus honoris sed ruinas animae plora (6)

The authors of these verses could have thought of Commodian's poetry only as doggerel. Their scholarship would tell them that he used false quantities; their instinct could not tell them that he used correctly the prosody of his own century:—so in imitating him they would naturally overlook the very essence of his art.

But the reason for Commodian's practice is, so far as our present inquiry is concerned, merely a question for the curious. The one fact of great present importance is that to Commodian the central point of interest and attention in his rhythm was the thesis of the metrical foot. He lived at a time when the native feeling for quantitative verse was all but gone;—but the verse still lived in its rhythm, by the force of its metrical ictus. Commodian has heretofore been regarded as the writer of an isolated type of verse, but it is now plain that he is directly in the line of our research. The particular path which he opened led nowhere, it is true, because it was based on an ephemeral condition of the language:—

---

(1) See Meyer pp. 276—284, and appendices.

but it gives as perfect a specimen as could be desired of the transition state between metric and rhythmic.

The other theory,—that these verses were of the syllabic order,—seemed indeed almost grotesque, for the essence of syllabism is equality, and here there is no equality:—and the writer has never been able to understand why the elements that were obvious should be lost and those that were not should be preserved.

An interesting corroboration of the foregoing argument is afforded by the passage in St. Augustine already referred to.(1) After the pupil has confessed himself baffled, the teacher says "At hoc mea pronuntiatione factum est, cum eo scilicet vitio quod barbarismum grammatici vocant: nam *primus* longa est et brevis syllaba; *primis* autem, ambae producendae sunt, sed ego ultimam earum corripui; *ita nihil fraudis passae sunt aures tuae*". Then the teacher repeats the verse in both forms, dwelling this time on the long *-is* in *primis*, and the pupil cries without hesitation, "Nunc vero negare non possum, nescio qua deformitate me offensum!"—He did not object to false quantities in the least, but his ear was offended by any hitch in the run of the line.(2)

---

(1) § 6, *ante.*

(2) It will be observed that the exact scansion of some lines, if considered by themselves, is doubtful: e. g. does the 1st line of the *Carm. Apol.* begin with a dactyl or a spondee? But the number of doubtful lines is minimized by Commodian's practice of putting his caesura after the thesis of the 3rd foot: thus if the 1st hemistich contains 7 syllables, it must contain 2 dactyls; if only 5 syllables, 2 spondees: its scansion is doubtful only if it contains just 6 syllables. So in the 2d hemistich there can be no doubt except where there are exactly 9 syllables. I have no doubt that this in the reason why Commodian divided his verses so uniformly. In doubtful cases we must choose that scansion which agrees with the system:—the system itself could be adequately established by examination of only those lines which are free from doubt.

CHAPTER III.
The Latin Hymns of Ambrose and his Followers.

§ 19. *Introductory remarks.* Commodian's verse was composed at a time when natural prosody still survived, through moribund. By the time of St. Augustine, however, as we have already seen, it was dead. While therefore the experiments of Commodian aimed to preserve the old rhythm in the last remnants of the old metrical garb, we should naturally expect later experimenters to discard the latter altogether, if they wished their verse to conform to the laws of ordinary pronunciation, and to find for the rhythm some other support than that of a forgotten prosody. This is exactly what was done, in the fifth and sixth centuries and after, by the writers of the Latin hymns. In the fourth century, Ambrose wrote the hymn beginning

> Jam surgit hora tertia
> Qua Christus adscendit crucem;
> Nil insolens mens cogitet,
> Intendat affectum precis.

Here we clearly have a quantitative metre, a scholarly reproduction of the classical iambic dimeter. Several centuries later, on the other hand, Adam of St. Victor was writing such verses as the following:

> Jesu, tuorum militum
> Transcendens omne meritum,
> Ad laudem tui militis
> Nos ejus juva meritis.

Here we at once see that there is no dependence upon quantity. The analogy of the 3rd and 8th century hexameters raises a strong presumption, however, that the apparent rhythm of the lines was designed; and if so, the verse is manifestly of the accentual order. Our task will be to ascertain how far this presumption is supported by the facts, and (if it proves justifiable) by what steps the new accentual system came in.

The hymns that have come down to us from the dark ages, exhibiting the change from quantitative to unquantitative structure in all its phases, afford more than enough material for solving the problem; but unfortunately something more is needed than abundance of material. Most of the specimens of verse in the interesting stages of transition are of very uncertain date. Thus the poem *De Gaudiis Paradisi*, of which the opening lines have already been quoted, has been variously ascribed to St. Augustine (354-430) and to Damiani (1002-1072), not to mention divers intermediate conjectures; and consequently, in an investigation to which accurate chronology is all-important, this hymn is practically useless. As might be expected, the authorship of the earliest hymns (i. e. those of the fourth, fifth and sixth centuries) is the most thickly befogged; and these, as it happens, are just the ones that exhibit the most interesting forms. There are a few, however, of the early hymns, which we can arrange in chronological order with entire confidence, and from these, and a few others, we shall be able to get some light upon our inquiry.

§ 20. *Ambrose.* About 385 A.D. Bishop Ambrose introduced in the church of Milan the singing of psalms and hymns. Many of these hymns were written by Ambrose himself, and many more, of similar style and metre, have been erroneously ascribed to him. Four are incontestably genuine,[1] namely "Deus Creator omnium",

---

[1] Being mentioned as his by St. Augustine.

"Aeterne rerum conditor", "Jam surgit hora tertia" and "Veni redemptor gentium". These are all composed in stanzas of four iambic dimeters, each constructed according to the common classical scheme, namely

$$\smile - | \smile - | \smile - | \smile -,$$

and all exhibit a fairly strict adherence to the traditions of quantity. In the first-named of the four there are two imperfect lines, namely

> Te diligat castus amor (15)
> and Ne hostis invidi dolo; (27)

in the second, there is one slight imperfection, in

> Jesu labentes respice; (25)

and similar irregularities may be found in the others; but in general quantity is respected, and of course (as the example given in the preceding section shows) there is no appearance of any regard for prose accent. From the teaching of Augustine we know that this form of composition involved a considerable degree of pedantry,—that it was governed by tradition rather than instinct;—and from the example of Commodian we can very well understand that what actually appealed to the ear in the reading of these hymns was not the quantity but the metrical ictus. Commodian avoided putting the ictus on any syllable which his senses felt to be short; Ambrose put it only on syllables which his erudition knew to be long.

§ 21. *Sedulius.* This poet (b. second half of 4th cent d. first half of 5th) wrote a hymn beginning "A solis ortus cardine". The hymn now extant with this beginning is thought to be only in part the work of Sedulius, but the whole hymn may properly be considered here as an early imitation of Ambrose.(1) The hymn is as strictly

---

(1) Although lines 13—24 are sometimes attributed to Ambrose himself: —see Julian's Dictionary.

quantitative as those of Ambrose himself, the irregularities being of the slightest kind, e. g.

Verbo concepit filium. (16)

The peculiarity of the hymn is this, that the authors have apparently sought, while observing quantity with scrupulous care, to attend to the prose accents also. The first three stanzas, for example, can be read accentually with perfect smoothness;—they will be found to contain no inversions except such as are common in modern English poetry.

> A solis ortus cardine
> Ad usque terrae limitem
> Christum canamus principem,
> Natum Maria virgine.
>
> Beatus auctor saeculi
> Servile corpus induit,
> Ut carne carnem liberans
> Ne perderet quos condidit.
>
> Castae parentis viscera
> Coelestis intrat gratia;
> Venter puellae bajulat
> Secreta quae non noverat.

An accentual reading of the whole hymn will, to be sure, exhibit more violent inversions than these, as for example in

Templum repente fit Dei (14)

or even   Et angeli canunt Deo. (26)

But these inversions are decidedly less noticeable than they would be in the hymns of Ambrose, similarly pronounced; and it is especially worthy of remark that in this Sedulian hymn the inversions always fall upon dissyllables. In all the 96 lines of the poem there is no polysyllable in which the metrical stress does not fall upon the accented syllable. That this would in all likelihood not be the case if it were not designed, is made sufficiently clear (without consideration of antecedent probability) by observation of the shorter hymns of Ambrose. In the first-named of the four already described we find

Et noctes exortu preces (10)

in the second,
> Hoc omnis errorum chorus (11)
> Pontique mitescunt freta (14)
> Et ore psallamus tibi (32)

in the third,
> Qua Christus adscendit crucem (2)
> Intendat affectum precis (4)
> Matri loquebatur suae (18)

and in the fourth
> Vexilla virtutum micant (11)
> Aequalis aeterno Patri. (21)

Although the authorship and date of "A solis ortus cardine" cannot be assigned with certainty from external evidence, the curious fact just noted seems to afford ground for a safe conjecture. Not long after the time of Sedulius a complete divorce had been consummated between rhythmic and metric. Thereafter those who wrote "rhythms" felt no scruple in disregarding quantity, and those who wrote in quantity recognized fully that their art was of the past not the present, and so could hardly care to struggle for an ineffectual compromise. This hymn, therefore, seems to have been composed, if not by Sedulius, at least by some one or more of his early followers, when the old system was still in the top of the fashion. They sought to keep it fresh by skilful doctoring.

§ 22. *Fortunatus.* There is at least one hymn, however, of unquestioned authorship, which exhibits the same peculiarity as that just discussed. This is the "Vexilla regis prodeunt" of Fortunatus (530-609 ?). That this hymn was composed with careful regard for quantity is evident from the consistent care with which the 3rd and 7th places in the verse are reserved for short syllables, the only slip being in

> Dicens in nationibus. (11)

This interesting hymn contains several verses which, if

read accentually, show the ordinary inversion of the first foot,—namely lines 10, 11, 13, 18, 22, 24 and 31. Three verses show inversions of a more serious nature, namely

>Fulget crucis mysterium (2)
>Regnabit a ligno Deus (12)
>O crux, ave, spes unica. (29)

But here, as in "A solis ortus cardine" there is no case of a polysyllable in which the normal ictus fails to coincide with the prose accent.

For convenience and brevity, dissyllabic words used with iambic stress have been spoken of as exhibiting "inversions". This is true only if the verses are read accentually, and it is of course not to be presumed that such a reading was ever intended by these early poets. We must, for the present, assume that such lines as

>Dicens in nationibus

were meant to be read with a regular alternation of arsis and thesis, and in them ictus and prose accent did not coincide. They exhibit the phenomenon known as "wrenched accent", rather than inversions of foot. But in the care with which the accent of polysyllables is preserved, there is a curious significance. Even to our modern ears, trained as they are to accentual rhythm, there is much less of the obviously conventional in such lines as those above quoted from Fortunatus, than in the

>Hoc omnis errorum chorus

or the   Matri loquebatur suae

of Ambrose: and it is evident that while the authors of the two hymns last described were anxious to respect the conventions of prosody they also were especially anxious not to thrust then into the foreground.

Further but perhaps more dubious evidence of the intention of these poets is found in the endings of their lines. In the hymn of Fortunatus only one line ends with a dissyllable:—that is to say, only one line fails to show concidence of ictus and accent at its end. In "A

solis ortus cardine", with a total of 96 lines, there are
9 dissyllabic endings. In the four hymns of Ambrose,
with a total of 124 lines, there are 37.(1).

§ 23. *Substitution of accent for prosodical length.* But
the most remarkable fact about this hymn of Fortunatus
has yet to be mentioned. Although the verse is for the
most part quantitative, as has been shown, there are two
lines in which, in defiance of the rules of quantity, short
syllables receive the metrical stress. These lines are

>Suspensus est patibulo (4)
>
>and Praedamque tulit tartari. (20)

Here the stressed short syllable is the one that bears the
prose accent. *Patibulum* is of course an impossible word
in pure iambics, but the 20th line could have been saved
by an easy transposition. The poet chose rather to let
a merely accented syllable stand for a long syllable,
than in either case to make any sacrifice of rhetorical
effectiveness. Fortunatus was of course consciously following what he believed to be the best fashion in sacred
composition. He imposed upon himself, for the nonce,
unusual restrictions, in the effort to secure coincidence of
accent with verse-ictus. He allowed himself frequently
to sacrifice the normal accent in the first foot of the
line; that was necessary, unless he would avoid dissyllabic beginnings, and it was comparatively unobjectionable: but he did not in general allow himself the same
liberty at the verse-end, although he had to forego dissyllabic endings to avoid it, for there it was not unobjectionable. In polysyllables, which could not be treated
lightly without a serious wrench, he adhered strictly to

---

(1) I state these facts because they exhibit the most vulnerable point
in this argument. There is no reason why wrenched accents should be
especially objectionable at the verse-end: cf. our English ballads. I can
explain the scruples of Fortunatus only by the consideration that rime and
"rhythm" were both new, and he treated them with the tenderness of
unfamiliarity.

the normal prose accent, and in two extreme cases he allowed this accent to usurp altogether the function of prosodical length.

§ 24. *Early hymns of uncertain date.* Here we seem to witness the last stage of transition, before the complete transformation of metre into rhythm. The hymns just considered afford at least *prima facie* reason for believing that the change was a natural and gradual one, that the rhythmical effect upon the unsophisticated ear was the same in each kind of verse, that the later hymns were not merely syllabic, but accentual, and that the change was begun by the device of making the metrical ictus of quantitative verse coincide with the prose accent of the words, and carried a step further by the substitution, at first only tentative, of accented for long syllables. The hymns of Ambrose and Fortunatus are the only ones in iambic metres which can with certainty be assigned to known authors of this transition period: and for reasons which will appear in the next chapter, the early hymns in quasi-trochaics cannot properly figure in the comparison. The materials are so scanty that our deductions cannot, of course, be regarded as independently conclusive; but it will be seen in the next chapters that their value can be greatly increased by corroborative evidence from other sources.

Many of the so-called Ambrosian hymns, (i. e. hymns in stanzas of four iambic dipodies, either metrical or "rhythmical"), and those attributed to Damasus and Hilary, would be of great value to the student of versification, if only he were in a position to speak confidently of their authorship and date. Those credited to the two authors named, if known to be authentic, would be of especial interest as being the oldest extant specimens of the Latin hymnology; but they are pretty certainly not authentic. To Damasus tradition ascribes the celebrated hymn on the martyrdom of Agatha, in dactylic verse:

>   Martyris ecce dies Agathae
>   Virginis emicat eximiae,
>   Christus eam sibi qua sociat
>   Et diadema duplex decorat.
>   5 Stirpe decens, elegans specie,
>   * * *
> 21 Jam renitens quasi sponsa polo, etc.

And to Hilary the hymn beginning "Lucis largitor splendide" is ascribed by his biographer Fortunatus, as well as by a fairly consistent tradition. This hymn (written for the most part strictly in quantity) contains two notable lines, namely

>   Ne rapientis perfidi (19)
>   and   Haec spes precantis animae (29).

The hymn of Damasus seems to reveal a comparative disregard of quantity in the arsis: for though the blunder in the 5th line might be purely accidental, the false quantity in *renitens* (or *renidens* according to other MSS.) cannot have been unnoticed, as the long penult controls the accent of the word. But though both these hymns (like divers others of similar character), could obviously be fitted into our theory very conveniently, the uncertainty of their true dates makes it unsafe to rely upon them. Both are later than the time of their supposed authors, but we cannot tell how much later except by reasoning in a circle. It is to be hoped that theological, literary and historical scholarship may before long clear up some of these questions, and so make considerable additions to the material now available for our present inquiry.

§ 25. *Ambrosian hymns of Adam of St. Victor.* Before considering the more complex features of the problem, it will be useful to examine the rhythm of the Ambrosian hymn in its last stage of development. Adam of St. Victor, the skilful (if hardly great) poet of the 12th century, was the most perfect master of Latin "rhythmical" composition, and has left many specimens of his work.

Among these are seven Ambrosian hymns. If these hymns are read accentually, they exhibit a strikingly large number of initial inversions, either single (i. e. of the first foot) as in "Jesu, tuorum militum", or double (i. e. of the first two feet together), as in "Felix ortus infantulae". The frequency of these inversions can be conveniently shown by the following table.

First line of hymn	Single inversions	Double	Total no. of lines
Lux illuxit Dominica	10	7	40
Genofevae solemnitas	12	16	52
Laudemus omnes inclyta	17	20	60
Aeterni festi gaudia	12	22	60
Supernae matris gaudia	7	15	52
Aurora diem nuntiat	6	5	23(1)
Jesu tuorum militum	7	4	23
Total	71	89	310

In somewhat more than half of the verses we find initial inversions, either single or double. But in all the 310 lines there are only two possible instances of inversion in the 3rd or 4th foot. These are both in the hymn "Aeterni festi gaudia", viz.:—

        Quae vellet potest mens pia (32)
and   Qua praefulget Augustinus (51)

In the former of these cases the inversion is obviously no inversion at all; the line is to be read with a wrenched accent. This is shown clearly enough by the fact that *pia* rimes with *omnia, scientia* and *caetera*. The latter case is doubtful. The whole stanza is as follows:—

        Datur et torques aurea
        Pro doctrina catholica:
        Qua praefulget Augustinus
        In summi regis curia.

In as much as the line in question does not rime, (contrary to the uniform rule of this hymn), it seems likely that the inversion is real, and that the poet de-

---

(1) The last line of this hymn, "Sancto sit spiritui", is defective, and I have not included it in the table. The same in true of the next hymn.

signedly introduced an entire trochaic line into this stanza: but of course the passage may be corrupt.

The frequency of initial inversions in such hymns as these seems to give color to the theory that the verse does not depend upon accent at all,—that it is in theory only syllabic. But the fact that the inversions are practically always initial—(there is no instance of inversion in the 2nd foot alone, unless possibly in l. 37 of the first hymn in the table, "O mors Christi mirifica)—seems strongly to negative this theory. It is perfectly true, of course, that final inversions would have prevented masculine rime; and the principle of systematic rime is the one principle that is admitted, in addition to that of syllabism, by those who uphold the theory that these verses are not accentual.(1) But this is no sufficient answer, for it is not clear how the principle of rime can be scientifically separated from that of accentual rhythm. If words like Marīa and marīa had been systematically treated as of equal fitness for the verse-end, we might regard the two principles as quite separate; but they in fact were not. Further confirmation of our view will be found in the next section: but for the present it may merely be remarked that the syllabic theory is that (for the most part) of French and German scholarship, and that our ears are perhaps readier to perceive the true character of these rhythms than those of the French and the Germans, because the latter are accustomed in their own poetry to a much more regular alternation of thesis and arsis than is found in ours, while the former, from the nature of their language, are hardly trained to appreciate an accentual rhythm at all.(2)

---

(1) See for example Kawczynski p. 117 *et seq.* It should perhaps be noted that the use of final monosyllables would have enabled the poet to invert the third foot alone without marring the rime, had he cared to do so.

(2) See for example a remarkable comment of Kawczynski's (p. 44). "Les poètes allemands qui imitèrent le vers octosyllabique des romans

It has been assumed in the foregoing paragraphs that these inversions in the poems of Adam are real inversions, not wrenched accents. That this is the case is clear enough from the fact that they occur only at the beginnings of lines. For that in accentual poetry an inverted foot is positively agreeable in the beginning, and in general positively disagreeable at the end of a verse, is clear enough; but no such assertion can be made as to wrenched accents. If a line like

Jesu dulcis memoria,

read with regular stress on the even syllables, was satisfactory to the ear, so would be such lines as

Te nostra vox primum sonet,(1)

Fortunatus to the contrary notwithstanding. And the comments of the grammarians, (see § 36, *post*), leave no doubt that these verses were read accentually.

§ 26. *Trochaics of Adam of St. Victor.* The opinion uged in the last section, as to the theoretical presence of the accentual principle in Adam's Ambrosian hymns, receives positive confirmation from his treatment of trochaic rhythms. Kawczynski says(2) (after arguing for the purely syllabic character of Latin "rhythms" in general):—"Il faut toutefois accorder une large exception au rhythme trochaïque. La langue latine ne possédant pas d'oxytons polysyllabiques, et les proparoxytons n'y

---

français ne parvinrent pas à donner à leurs vers un nombre de syllabes déterminé. Cela les gênait trop probablement. En voici la règle exprimée par un rimeur du quatorzième siècle:

Ouch ich diss getichniss rim
Uef die zal der silben zune,
Sechse, sibene, achte, nune.

Il rime son écrit, dit-il, sur le nombre des syllabes, dix, sept, huit ou neuf. *Le seul rhythme qu'on donnait à ces vers consistait donc dans la rime.* (!)

(1) From the *"Aeterne rerum conditor"* of Ambrose.
(2) p. 119.

étant pas très nombreux,(1) la cadence trochaïque est très fréquente et toute naturelle aux mots latins. Il y a donc beaucoup de vers latins rhythmiques dans lesquels elle est presque régulièrement maintenue par les accents, mais dans les meilleures pièces, même de ce genre, on trouvera toujours quelques vers où elle est brisée, bien qu'une légère transposition des mots eût suffi pour la rétablir. Elle n'était donc pas obligatoire, elle n'entrait pas dans la notion et dans la définition des vers rythmiques". But an examination of the hymns of Adam, which are certainly among "les meilleures pièces", will show that the regular trochaic cadence *was* obligatory and did enter most essentially into the poet's conception of the rhythm. The exceptions referred to by Kawczynski are of that rare sort which really do prove the rule.

To make the character of this verse clear a careful examination has been made of some of Adam's hymns. A number were selected at random:—namely the seven hymns on the Nativity, which are given first in the recent editions. The results of this examination may be conveniently tabulated as follows:—

First line of hymn	No. of inversions	Total no. of lines
Potestate, non natura	3	56
In excelsis canitur	8	58
In natale Salvatoris	4	70(2)
Lux est orta gentibus	2	12
Jubilemus Salvatori	2	24
Nato nobis Salvatore	2	30
Splendor Patris et figura	7	68
Total	28	318

Here we see that while inversions occur in more than

---

(1) M. Kawczynski has evidently not resorted to the mechanical device of counting them!

(2) There are 76 lines in the hymn, but ll. 49, 50 and 54—57 form a sort of interlude in a different kind of rhythm. Parts of this hymn are repeated in the next two, and I have therefore only reckoned those parts of the latter which are new.

one half of Adam's iambic lines, they are found in less than one eleventh of his trochaics. A typical specimen will illustrate the character of the inverted trochee. The second hymn begins as follows:—

> In excelsis canitur
> Nato regi gloria,
> Per quem terrae redditur
> Et coelo concordia.

Now the comparative infrequency of these inversions might be partly accounted for by Kawczynski's explanation of the trochaic character of the Latin language, though it is hard to see how that could effect a discrepancy, such as we find here, of 83 per cent. But there is a curious uniformity in the character of these inversions which his theory does not account for at all. The seven hymns in question consist in the main of lines of 8 and 7 syllables. The octosyllabics are decidedly the more common, Adam's favorite stanza-form being a combination of four or six of the longer lines with two of the shorter. The former have a feminine ending, the latter a masculine, as the first lines of the hymns in the table show. Now there is obviously no reason in the supposed trochaic character of the Latin language why such inversions as occur in the first two feet of these lines should happen to be more common in one form than in the other; but as a matter of fact all the 28 inversions shown in the table do occur in the first two feet, and of these all but two are in the lines of 7 syllables.(1)

---

(1) I doubt if these two are real inversions after all. They occur in the hymn "In natale Salvatoris", and are as follows:—*Harmonia diversorum* (4), and *Post Deum spes singularis* (60). The latter is easily accounted for as exhibiting a wrenched accent, — which as all students of the subject know, was particularly common with the word *Deus*, as with most proper names. The former line may indicate that *harmonia* was accented on the penult after the analogy of the Greek ἁρμονία. This sort of accentuation was very common, and the fact that Adam uses *harmonia* as a proparoxytone in l. 2 of his familiar hymn "Aeterni festi gaudia" determines nothing; for the Greek word εἴδωλον for example was represented in Late Latin by either *idŏlum* or *idōlum* indifferently.

The true reason for the comparative infrequency of inversions in these trochaic lines is not hard to find. It lies not in the character of the language, but in the different characters of the two rhythms. The iambic admits inversions easily, the trochaic does not. It is well understood that in English verse, for example, there is a natural tendency toward the iambic run, and if it is desired to keep a measure trochaic in the main, it must be kept so throughout: while an iambic measure can be frequently interrupted by trochees without serious disturbance. Any one who is not familiar with this fact can satisfy himself of it by counting the number of inversions in any trochaic English poem (as for example *Locksley Hall*), and comparing his results with the number found in any passage of good blank verse.

The particular type to which all these inversions in Adam of St. Victor's trochaic hymns belong, is, as it happens, almost unknown in English verse, and at first glance it seems more divergent than it really is, from the normal. If a number of them are examined without their context, as

> Et coelo concordia,
> De carne puerperae,
> Coelesti praeconio,
> Sub noctis silentio,

they look as if they ran with a sort of anapæstic movement, (or perhaps like dactylic dimeters with anacrusis), and so understood they threaten seriously to mar the general harmony of the verse: but if they are read carefully as proper trochaics with only the first foot inverted, the effect will generally be found far from displeasing, even to our unaccustomed ears. Thus instead of

> Coelés | ti praecó | nio,

or

> Coe | lésti prae | cónio,

read

> Coelés | ti prae | cóni | o,

and the line will fit its context. The effect is substantially reproduced in English in a stanza from *The Vision of Sin*:

> Trooping from their mouldy dens
> The chap-fallen circle spreads:
> Welcome, fellow citizens,
> Hollow hearts and empty heads!

§ 27. *The invention of the initial inversion.* The analogy, then, of Adam's trochaics removes all doubt as to the presence of the accentual principle in his iambics. Such of his lines as are strictly regular must be viewed not as happy accidents, but as exhibiting the normal verse-form: those which show initial inversions, on the other hand, are not to be regarded as equally representative of a supposed merely syllabic type, but are interruptions to the smooth flow of the ideal rhythm. They occur often enough to prevent monotony; but constant recurrence to the type keeps the latter always in the reader's mind.(1)

But while it cannot be doubted that these late Latin rhythms were read generally according to their accents, with frequent initial inversions, it is almost equally clear, as we have seen, that the irregularities in the first tentative efforts at accentual verse must have been regarded not as inversions but as wrenched accents; - for the ideal rhythm of the quantitative iambic verse was perfectly regular in the time of Ambrose, and that ideal rhythm was the element of the old verse that suggested the invention of the new. Inversions of foot, in the sense

---

(1) The same inversions occur in English octosyllabics, but they are in comparison with the Latin very rare. In our heroic verse they are of course common. I have not yet been able to satisfy myself positively as to the reason for the difference between our octosyllabics and the Latin, but it must probably be found in some practical difference in the two modes of speech. A suggestive clue may perhaps be found in the general regularity of the German decasyllabic verse, as compared with ours. Compare, however, the note on the pronunciation of Latin, § 44, *post*.

in which we have been using the term, were unknown to the writers of quantitative iambic dipodies, and when they were first introduced they must have seemed a very radical innovation. The history of the transformation of metric into rhythmic cannot be regarded as fully ascertained until the time and manner of this innovation have been determined: but it must be admitted, though with reluctance, that with the present dearth of material no conclusive evidence on these points can be obtained.

Clues are to be found, to be sure. For example, in the quantitative pseudo-Hilarian hymn "Lucis largitor splendide", the lines

>Cujus admota gratia, (15)
>Nostra patescunt corpora (16)

and Ne rapientis perfidi (19)

exhibit interesting peculiarities in quantity:—for not only is the second syllable short in each case;—but the first syllable is long. And moreover in the first two cases, [and perhaps in all three(1)], the initial feet are not only quantitative trochees, but accentual trochees also. If phenomena of this sort could be assigned to a definite period, (say between the dates of Sedulius and Fortunatus) a solution of the problem might be obtained from them: but unfortunately they cannot be assigned to any date.

Another clue, perhaps not quite so faint, is found in the treatment of polysyllables in the anonymous early Ambrosian hymns. The writer has made, for this purpose, an examination of six(2) of these hymns: namely "Jesu nostra redemptio", "Hymnum dicamus Domino", "Christe

---

(1) A slight rhetorical emphasis on *ne* will of course obliterate the secondary accent in *rapientis*. Compare, however, the view of this line suggested in § 24, *ante*.

(2) I have of course made the selection quite at random, so far as fitness for the argument is concerned. For convenience of reference I chose those six of the Ambrosian hymns given in March's "*Latin Hymns*" which are clearly not intended to be quantitative.

qui lux es et dies", "Aurora lucis rutilat", "O Rex aeterne Domine", and "Mediae noctis tempus est". In the first of these hymns, which is probably the oldest, (having been persistently, though of course erroneously, ascribed to Ambrose himself), there are no polysyllables in which the regular accent does not coincide with the normal metrical stress. In the last named of the six, which is probably also the latest,(1) there are 8. In all the hymns together there are 18 such polysyllables, in a total of 236 lines. A decided majority of these (13) occur in the first halves of their respective lines, so that that those lines, if read accentually, present only the familiar initial versions, single or double. E. g. in the second of the hymns named we have

     Oscula petit Dominum (14)
  and Innocens et innoxius (19)
but also Fallaces Judaei impii (25)

and in the third we have

     Oculi somnum capiant (13)
     Dextera tua protegat (15)
  and Famulos qui te diligunt (16).

It looks very much as if these polysyllables, where their accent affects only the first foot, or the first two feet, were meant to be read as in prose,—otherwise (perhaps) to be forced into the regular rhythmical scheme. If this can be believed, it would seem that at a very early date,—as soon as the accentual principle was fairly grasped,—the propriety and beauty of occasional inversions came to be appreciated. We should then explain the verses of Fortunatus somewhat differently: for his irregularities could be called ordinary inversions. His

---

(1) See March's note: he assigns it to the 6th century. I should think, from the irregularities in the numbers of syllables (ll. 33, 34) and the intermixture of trochaic lines (ll. 46, 47) that it must be as late as that. It could hardly have been written before the accentual idea was firmly grasped.

hymn would then be regarded not as written in quantity, with careful observance of prose accents, but as written accentually, with all convenient regard for the rules of quantity. This, indeed, seems the more plausible view, but in the present state of our knowledge it is hard to see how any certain inferences can be drawn.

CHAPTER IV.
Early Church Music. Syllabic verse.

§ 28. *Introduction.* The opinion advanced in the foregoing pages as to the origin and nature of the late Latin rhythmical versification is of course too obvious to be wholly novel,(1) but lately, in the search for more remote explanations, its obviousness has become obscured. The purpose of this chapter will be to explain away one of the most serious misunderstandings by which students have been led away from the plain path. There are in existence several specimens of late Latin verse of a strictly syllabic character, in which even the most strenuous upholder of the accentual theory can find no trace of the accentual principle. These have been regarded as proving (by obvious analogy) the absence of that principle from other forms of verse:(2)—but it is believed that they can easily be explained as not inconsistent with the accentual theory. Most of the early "rhythmical" verse was meant to be sung, and sufficient attention has not been paid—in the investigation of the "rhythms" themselves—to the exigencies of the music which accompanied them. It is believed that a consideration of the diverse styles of music in use in the early churches will materially aid the present investigation.

---

(1) See, for example, Gautier, I. 281 et seq., where similar conclusions are reached, though by somewhat questionable reasoning.

(2) Cf. Meyer's treatment of Augustine's Psalm.

Our information about early Christian music is scanty. "However persevering" says Fétis(1) "may be the historian's efforts to collect information about the music of the Roman church during the first four centuries, they must result only in a conviction of their futility, for no trustworthy document on that subject is now extant. A few words of Tertullian, dealing in generalities too vague to be of any use to us, are all that we can cite". It would seem, therefore, that most of what we can learn about the music of this period must be by inference from what we know of the state of music before the Christian era and of the state of music after the fourth century: but we shall find that there is some contemporary evidence which, though indirect, will be of no mean value.

§ 29. *Greek music.* Fortunately the aspect of the subject that is most nubilous is one which does not concern our present inquiry at all,—namely, the question as to the modes and keys employed in the early churches. The various modes in vogue at different times seem to have had none but the most indirect effect upon the time and rhythm of the melodies. These latter are the elements with which versification is most intimately connected, and they can be studied independently, so far as they need now be studied at all.

The most striking characteristic of the religious melodies composed by the Greeks immediately before our era was this, that they followed closely, in time, the quantities of the syllables to which they were sung.(2) A long note was not sung to a short syllable, nor *vice versa*:—and in general each syllable was represented by a single note in the melody. A few measures from one

---

(1) Vol. 4, p. 147. Tertullian's valueless testimony is given on p. 5 of the same volume.

(2) The contrary view was formerly held, on the authority of a passage in Dionysius of Halicarnassus:—See Chappell, I. p. 172. But cf. also Monro, p. 117.

of the musical inscriptions recently exhumed at Delphi will make this clear.

ἵ-να Φοῖ-βον ᾧ - δαῖ-σιμέλ-ψη-τε χρυ-σε-ο-κό-μαν.

Here the two circumflexed syllables take two notes each. This is usually the case throughout the hymn, and in a few instances long syllables that are not circumflexed are treated similarly; but there is a general correspondence of note for syllable, and the musical time and rhythm agree *always* with the prosody. That this was universally the case admits no doubt. Changes in time may have been common,(2)—changes in tempo perhaps still more so,—but words and music would of course be affected by such changes exactly alike.

The fragment given above dates probably from the 3rd century, B. C.(3) The other musical inscriptions discovered with it at Delphi are much shorter and more imperfect. They appear to be of much later date, the most considerable of them belonging apparently to the 1st century B. C. They present the same characteristics as the one just discussed, except that in the first place the time-values of the notes in one fragment undergo the changes necessary to fit them to a logaœdic measure, and in the second place the custom of suiting each syllable with a single note appears to have become a rule without exceptions. Even the circumflexed syllables have but one note apiece.

§ 30. *The music of Ambrose.* It is to be wished that authentic specimens might be given of Roman music

---

(1) I copy part of the transcription given by Monro, p. 136.
(2) Cf. Aristoxenus Fragm. Ed. Marquardt, p. 48.
(3) Monro, p. 134.

composed in the early days of the empire; but even without such specimens it seems certain that in at least the two particulars specified (the correspondence of note with syllable and of time with quantity) the accomplished musicians of Rome copied their Greek predecessors. Belief in this is justified by the familiar phenomena of Latin lyrical measures, by the practical monopoly which the Greeks enjoyed in the profession of music-teaching at Rome, and finally by the absence of any ground for suspecting the contrary.

We have therefore a right to assume, provisionally, that in the 4th century of our era the hymns of Ambrose were sung to music which possessed much the same character. Being written in a measure borrowed from the lyric poets of paganism, it seems most probable that these hymns were designed for melodies such as those poets had used. It has been objected that, according to Augustine, Ambrose borrowed the idea of his hymns from "the Eastern church" and that the music of the Eastern churches at this time was by no means descended from that of pagan Greece. But what Augustine says on this subject is as follows:—"Justina, the mother of the boy emperor Valentinian, persecuted Thy servant Ambrose in the interest of her heresy. * * * The pious people kept guard in the church, prepared to die with their bishop, Thy servant. There my mother, Thy handmaid, bearing a chief part of those cares and watchings, lived in prayer. * * * At this time it was instituted that after the manner of the Eastern church, hymns and psalms should be sung, lest the people should pine away in the tediousness of sorrow".(1) There is nothing in this about an importation of a foreign system of music: it appears only that the idea of singing hymns at all was borrowed. Indeed the passage seems to tell strongly

---

(1) Aug. Conf. IX. 7. 15 (Pilkington's translation).

against the view referred to, for it shows that the earliest Latin hymns were designed expressly for general congregational use. That Ambrose should have asked his devoted followers, for their own relief and encouragement, to sing hymns to a style of music with which they were wholly unacquainted, is as unlikely as that a modern revivalist should lead a miscellaneous meeting in the choruses of sacred music from Tannhäuser and Parsifal. It is much more probable,—indeed it is almost certain,— that Ambrose would adapt for the purposes of his church, the same style of music that had been taught for several centuries in Italy.(1)

§ 31. *Music of the Roman Empire in general.* Thus far, then, it seems probable that in the Ambrosian music there was a more or less strict correspondence of note with syllable, and that the music was rhythmical, with its beat (in iambic measures) on the long syllables. But it is necessary to observe that the citizens of the Roman empire were by no means all of one practice in the matter of music. It is well known that in later days the usage of Milan and the usage of Rome were very dissimilar; and as for the earlier days, the very fact that Greek teachers of music were in such demand indicates a strong individuality in the Greek system. There must have been marked differences between the practices of tutored and untutored Italy, in the first centuries of the empire, and it is perhaps doubtful whether the Greek system ever reached all classes. The Christians who through the generations of persecution were meeting in

---

(1) From Ptolemy it appears that sweeping changes were made after the time of Aristoxenus,—chiefly tending towards simplification,—in standard Greek music (cf. Monro, p. 78):—but they seem to have affected only the keys and modes, leaving melodic principles untouched. The traditions of weird chromatic appoggiaturas, &c., in Ambrosian music, are not authenticated; but such embellishments, if they did exist, must have been mostly extra-metrical.

the secret chambers of the Catacombs are known to have had their music,—their "psalms and hymns and spiritual songs". To what sort of melodies these were sung we can probably never know exactly, but there is reason enough for believing that it was of a different character from that just described. The Christian religion had little to do, in those days, with fashion and the fine arts, and even in Italy the Greek culture may well have failed to reach it. As to other parts of the Empire, the antecedent probability is still stronger. The apostles did not travel as music teachers, and whatever their own native prejudices may have been, they did not enforce them upon their followers. If the words sung expressed a heartfelt Christian faith, it made little difference what modes or melodies were used with them. The styles of the early Christians at Rome, and elsewhere about the Mediterranean, were of a thoroughly popular character, we can be sure, simple and doubtless often crude; and where Latin was the native language, the music could hardly concern itself long with verbal prosody: but beyond that we can in general only conjecture from what we know of later developments(1).

§ 32. *St. Augustine's Psalm.* An interesting light, however, is thrown upon the character of the music in at least one part of the empire, by Augustine's *Psalmus contra Donatistas.* It will be remembered that from 395 to 430 Augustine was Bishop of Hippo. This psalm was written for didactic purposes, and was intended to make clear to the congregation the fallacies of the Donatist heresy, then rife in Numidia. We are fortunate in having Augustine's own account of the poem, viz:—
"Volens etiam causam Donatistarum ad ipsius humillimi vulgi et omnino imperitorum atque idiotarum notitiam

---

(1) The substance of this paragraph is largely taken from Ambros, II. 9—11, and Fétis, IV. 8.

pervenire et eorum quantum fieri posset per nos inhaerere memoriae, psalmum qui eis cantaretur per latinas litteras feci. * * * * Iste psalmus sic incipit: Omnes qui gaudetis".(1) That is to say, he purposely adapted his psalm to the intellectual abilities, and undoubtedly also to the musical appreciativeness, of Christians of the lowest order of culture. The psalm itself begins as follows:—

> Omnes qui gaudetis [de] pace, modo verum judicate.
> Abundantia peccatorum solet fratres conturbare:
>   propter hoc Dominus noster voluit nos praemonere
>   comparans regnum coelorum reticulo misso in mare,
>   congreganti multos pisces, omne genus, hic et inde.
> Quos quum traxissent ad litus, tunc coeperunt separare,
>   bonos in vasa miserunt, reliquos malos in mare.
> Quisquis novit Evangelium, recognoscat cum timore:
> videt reticulum ecclesiam, videt hoc saeculum mare.

Of this style of versification St. Augustine himself says "Non aliquo carminis genere id fieri volui, ne me necessitas metrica ad aliqua verba quae minus sunt usitata compelleret". In order to secure perfect simplicity, he was able to dispense with prosody: and it is evident that the music known to the church at Hippo demanded neither metre nor rhythm in the words.

But there are elements of regularity in the psalm. There are 285 verses in all, and each one [with some dozen exceptions(2)] contains 16 syllables with a caesura after the 8th. Vowels are generally not elided at the caesura, though they are elsewhere almost uniformly. Each verse (except a few that are undoubtedly corrupt)

---

(1) Retractationum, l. 1. c. 20.

(2) In the text printed by Du Méril, I. 120, I noted four exceptional lines, two of 17 and two of 15 syllables each. [Of course the synizesis in Evangelium (4 syllables) and Ecclesiam (3 syllables) presents no difficulty]. Several verses, however, are made regular only by Du Méril's conjectural emendations. The careful examination of the Benedictine text made by Meyer (q. v. p. 20 et seq.) shows 21 irregular lines:—but this number is too liberal, as it includes several cases in which an obvious syncope is all that is needed to make the line normal.

ends with a paroxytone; so also do most of the first hemistichs: but there is no further accentual regularity. Each line ends with the vowel e, thus riming crudely with all the rest. By the frequent recurrence of the first line the whole poem is divided into stanzas, which are further distinguished by the alphabetical consecutiveness of their initial letters. Each of these stanzas contains an even number of verses, (either 10 or 12), and at the end there is a concluding passage of 30 verses.(1)

§ 33. *The music of Augustine's Psalm.* Now as Augustine was clearly not striving for poetical effectiveness, these various elements of regularity must have been introduced for the sake of the music;—and they seem to show pretty plausibly what the general style of that music was. There must, in the first place, have been a very thorough correspondence of note for syllable and syllable for note, or the syllabic structure of the verse would hardly have been maintained so rigidly;—it was certainly of no intrinsic value. Secondly, the music must have been neither prosodical nor strongly rhythmical; in other words it was probably so slow and sustained that it made no difference, as the notes dragged along, whether the syllables that accompanied them were long or short, accented or unaccented. Thirdly, the music, though so unrhythmical in general movement, must have taken the form of some sort of tune, or melodic progression, which was repeated or at least imitated after every second verse. And lastly, there seems to have been something like a rhythmical cadence, involving the last two or three notes of each bar, which relieved the melody of its creeping monotony.

---

(1) These facts are stated in substance by Du Méril and in detail by Meyer. The careful analysis given by the latter makes it unnecessary for me to state more than the general results of my own examination of the psalm.

That this was the character of the music is perhaps not conclusively proved by the versification of the psalm:— but the probability amounts to more than a reasonable hypothesis, for no other hypothesis affords a satisfactory explanation of the verse. The unrhythmical nature of the music in general is all the more probable because of the care with which verbal rhythm is secured at the verse-end, where the music would naturally, in any case, be somewhat rhythmical. A cadence-effect would indeed be produced at the end of the bar by the mere occurrence of a pause after the hemistich, for the ear in such a case is forced to dwell on the last two or three notes and make a cadence of them, even when they are actually equal in time and stress; and that such a pause occured here is clear from the author's practice in the matter of elision: but the rime at the verse-end, and the almost uniform feminine endings of the hemistichs show that in fact the verse-end was still more strongly marked, and of course the music corresponded. It is a significant feature of the verse that where verbal rhythm was demanded it was secured not by quantity but by accent. (See the short accented penult in *mare* l. 4 of the extract.) To Augustine, as to Sedulius and Fortunatus, verbal accent was the natural concomitant of rhythmical ictus, wherever such ictus needed verbal reinforcement at all.

Other compositions in verse of the same character as that just described are best explained in the same way. As a single additional specimen of such verse it may be interesting to refer to the ancient hymn in honor of St. Patrick.(1) It begins as follows:—

    Audite omnes amantes Deum, sancta merita
       viri in Christo beati, Patrici episcopi;
       quomodo bonum ob actum similatur angelis,
       perfectamque propter vitam aequatur apostolis.

---

(1) Found in an 8th cent. MS.:—said in Julian's Dict. to have been composed perhaps about 458, but I do not know upon what authority this conjecture rests.

> Beati Christi custodit mandata in omnibus,
>   cujus opera refulgent clara inter homines,
>   sanctumque cujus sequuntur exemplum mirificum,
>   unde et in coelis patrem magnificant Dominum.

The two hemistichs of each line are of 7 and 8 syllables respectively, and are neither quantitative nor accentual,—except that the poet shows a preference for a feminine ending in the first hemistich and for a masculine ending in the second. The hymn is divided (according to the letters of the alphabet) into stanzas of four lines each. Elision does not occur at all in the two quatrains given above, and it is rare in the rest of the poem.

§ 34. *The two schools of church music.* It has been shown that antecedent probability, and the evidence of two distinct kinds of verse in the early hymns, favor the theory that there were in the 4th century two kinds of music in common use. That which prevailed at Milan perpetuated the traditions of Greek culture. It was taken up by the church at a time when Christianity was no longer vulgar; and we have seen from Augustine's autobiography that the congregation included at least one woman of exceptional culture. This music seems to demand a verbal rhythm in whatever verses were set to it. But at the same time, there seems to have been another style, prevailing elsewhere, which made no such demand.

But the existence of two styles of music in the early church is a matter of history; and the evidence of tradition, as well as that of later musical development, points to just such a distinction between them as has here been drawn. The two styles are commonly known as the use of Milan and the use of Rome, and are associated with the names of the two great reformers, Ambrose and Gregory, respectively. Without reviewing in detail the *a posteriori* arguments of the historians of music, it remains only to cite their testimony as to the general results.

In Fétis's Dictionary we find the following:(1)—"La prosodie et le rhythme paraissent avoir disparu de la langue latine chantée au temps de Saint Grégoire: on croit qu'il acheva de l'effacer, et que, dans son antiphonaire, toutes les syllabes étaient notées à temps égaux". And again:(2) "La distinction entre le chant grégorien et l'ambroisien consista donc ordinairement, d'une part, en ce que celui de saint Ambroise était la tradition du chant de l'église grecque, avec ses ornements et l'usage de certaines suites de sons chromatiques, * * * tandis que la réforme de saint Grégoire fit disparaitre ces successions de sons étrangères au chant diatonique; d'autre part, le chant ambroisien était rhythmique, et le grégorien ne l'était pas. Mais par la suite des temps, ces différences essentielles ont disparu, et depuis plusieurs siècles on n'apercoit plus de distinction saississable entre ces formes du chant ecclésiastique."

The obvious explanation of the so-called reforms of Gregory is well stated by Apel as follows:(3)—"Was sogleich in die Sinne fällt, dass nämlich der accentuirte Gesang, der sich in Hauptmomenten bewegt, weit mehr geeignet ist von grossen Volksmassen gesungen zu werden, als der quantitirende, weil jener ungebildeten Stimmen zu Hilfe kommt, die sich bloss dem kunstlosen Naturgefühl von Arsis und Thesis zu überlassen brauchen, und überdies grosse Tonmassen sich allezeit anständiger und würdevoller in gleichen Zeiträumen fortbewegen als in ungleichzeitigen: dieses bemerkte auch Gregorius und begründete auf diese Bemerkung seinen Plan zur Reformation des Kirchengesanges."

---

(1) Fétis Dict. s. n. Grégoire.
(2) Ib. s. n. Ambroise. This is curiously inconsistent in some respects with *dicta* in Fétis' history:—but there is such a general unanimity on the main point at issue, among the best authorities, that it has seemed not worth while to re-open the questions involved.
(3) II. § 498, as quoted by Ambros, II. 60.

And finally the most scholarly of all the recent treatises on this subject contains the following:(1) "Man pflegt, wie gesagt, den Unterschied zwischen dem Ambrosianischen und dem Gregorianischen Gesange wesentlich darin zu suchen, dass jener Längen und Kürzen unterschieden, dieser die unterschiedlos gleiche Dauer aller einzelnen Töne eingeführt habe. Richtiger hiesse es vielleicht: dass der Ambrosianische Gesang wesentlich auf der poetischen, der Gregorianische auf der musikalischen Metrik beruhte. * *. * Die eigentliche Bedeutung der Gleichdauer der Bewegung des Gregorianischen Gesanges liegt aber nicht in dem taktmässigen, gleichlangen Aushalten jeder Note, sondern (im Gegensatz gegen die metrischen, d. i. die prosodische Eigenschaft jeder Silbe zur Geltung bringenden Gesänge) darin, dass an sich alle Sylben ohne Rücksicht auf Prosodie für völlig gleichbedeutend, für isometrisch genommen werden, und daher nach den Bedürfnissen des Rhythmus die prosodisch lange Silbe auch in der Geltung einer kurzen genommen werden kann und umgekehrt, und bloss die Gesetze der natürlichen Declamation zu berücksichtigen sind."

Here it is to be observed that there are some striking differences of opinion as to matters of detail. Ambros by no means believes that the music of Gregory's celebrated antiphonary was wholly unrhythmical:—and Fétis thinks that the style of Milan, though strictly prosodical, was distinguished by a much more lavish use of musical ornament. But as to these essential facts their conclusions are the same:—that the Ambrosian music was rhythmical, and necessitated verbal prosody, but that the Gregorian, whether rhythmical in itself or not, made no such demands upon the verse.

§ 35. *The influence of the church music on versification.* Ancient tradition has it that Gregory's system

---

(1) Ambros, II. 59-61.

was not a new invention, but largely a compilation and revision of systems that had prevailed in the early churches: his object was not to introduce a new system, but to reduce to uniformity the diverse practices of different communities.(1) As to the most distinctive feature of his system, it is evident from what has gone before that this tradition must be correct; for St. Augustine's psalm shows that this feature, though perhaps in a much cruder form, was familiar as early as the 4th century. As it was apparently popular in Augustine's time, it may well have existed from the beginning of our era, or even earlier.

The significance of all this is apparent enough. During the 4th, 5th and 6th centuries, which as we have already seen witnessed the transformation of metrical into rhythmical verse, two radically different styles of music were in vogue. One style was at first strictly prosodical, and always strongly rhythmical. The other was so unrhythmical (or, as Ambros would say, so independent of verbal rhythm) that even in the days when prosody was not yet a thing of the past, it could and did disregard it. The former style (the Ambrosian) was strict in its demands upon the verse, for it was at first only by a prosodical correspondence between words and music that the difficulties of the music could be overcome: hence we find a class of hymns in which, as prosody died out, regular accentual versification took its place. The old prosody could be discarded, for the new rhythm answered the same purpose better. Later still, as the unified system of Gregory began more and more to assert itself throughout the church, the stricter iambic rhythm might, so far as the music was concerned, be dispensed with, and the poet would need to practice only what he had learned about euphony of verse, without

---

(1) Ambros, II. 43, 44, and esp. the authorities cited p. 43, n.

reference to musical exigencies:—and it is probably at this time that the wrenched accent yielded to the inverted foot.

The Gregorian style, on the other hand, or rather that style which afterwards was associated with the name of Gregory, made no such demands on the verse. Whether or not it possessed some sort of slow and stately rhythm, it was at least easy for choirs to sing it without verbal prompting, and so adequate verses could be written for it without much regard for either prosody or accentual rhythm. The Gregorian style required that the verse should be strictly syllabic, for note and syllable must correspond; but it did not, like the Ambrosian, require the verse to be rhythmical also.

We are now in a position to discern the error into which students of this subject have fallen. Meyer, having failed to discover the true principle of Commodian's verse, was led to believe that in the change from metric to "rhythmic" only the syllabic principle survived. He asserted that this was the case even in the so-called rhythmical hexameters, where upon his own showing the first hemistich contains either 5, 6 or 7 syllables, and the second either 8, 9 or 10. Next he observed that all the Latin "rhythmical" verses (or nearly all) exhibit the syllabic principle in rigorous application, while some of them show an apparent accentual structure and others do not. His natural conclusion was that the syllabic principle was the essential thing in all, and that where an accentual rhythm seemed to show itself it was merely accidental. The true explanation is already too clear to need re-statement.

Meyer is not content, it is true, with the assumption of mere survival of the syllabic principle from the classical verse-forms. He contends that the Latin poets adopted from the Oriental literatures the discovery that this principle was sufficient in itself to build verses upon.

The present writer is not familiar enough with this branch of the subject to criticize the argument in detail,(1) but it is certainly unnecessary. St. Augustine, for example, needed no foreign model. As we have seen, he apologized for not writing any real kind of verse. The kind of verse which he thought might have been expected of him was doubtless a form of the trochaic tetrameter: it would have been both quantitative and syllabic. As, however, Augustine was not writing poetry for its own sake, he dropped the quantitative element altogether; but he kept his lines strictly syllabic because he had to. Those of the Ambrosian hymns which contain complex inversions might possibly be regarded as imitated from foreign models; or, perhaps more plausibly, they might be regarded as due to the influence of such syllabic verse as that of Augustine's psalm:—but, as we have seen, it is much easier to regard them not as evidences of the naked presence of the syllabic principle, but rather as mere euphonious varieties of the accentual type.

§ 36. *Contemporary accounts of the Latin rhythms.* Kawczynski, in his very interesting treatise on the Latin rhythms, has followed Meyer to very similar conclusions. Only one branch of his argument needs to be touched here. By copious quotations from early grammarians and rhetoricians he maintains the thesis that his (and Meyer's) conception of the Latin rhythms was also the conception of the scholars of the period under discussion. There is something, perhaps, of scholastic nicety in Kawczynski's argument, but it nevertheless seems at first sight formidable. It is clear, however, that a form of verse which arose after the middle of the 4th century, cannot be satis-

---

(1) Except that as to the prominent part which he assigns to the Hebrew poetry in the Latin movement Meyer must certainly be wrong. The latest results of Hebrew scholarship seem to negative the idea of any syllabic structure in the Jewish psalmody.

factorily explained by the definitions of grammarians who were then dead. Thus when Diomedes, in the 3th century, says "Rhythmus est pedum temporumque junctura cum levitate sine modo",(1) we are inclined to doubt whether this definition was framed after actual observation of such verses as we are considering; we are tempted to explain it rather as an unthinking repetition of a subtle distinction made by the Greek and Alexandrine theorists: and in any case, it tells us no more than we have already learned from Augustine's psalm.

The only real difficulty to be encountered in Kawczynski's quotations,—and that not a serious one,— is the persistent application, by theorists after the time of transition, of the same old word "rhythmus" to the new phenomena of what we now call rhythmical verse. Thus one of his quotations is from the venerable Bede (675—735 A. D.), viz:—"Videtur autem rhythmus esse metris consimilis, quae est verborum modulata compositio non metrica ratione sed numero syllabarum ad judicium aurium examinata, ut sunt carmina vulgarium poetarum".(2) Here the word is certainly applied to the kind of verse that we have been discussing. Does its use signify that Bede saw nothing more in it than is set forth in the definition of Diomedes?

Here we might fairly take refuge in the belief that novelties in art can be better explained, in their theoretical aspect, by the students of a later age than by contemporaries. With a dozen centuries of accentual poetry to study, we are less likely to misunderstand the sub-conscious purposes of its originators than were those who had the simple advantage of living with them. But we are by no means driven to rely entirely upon this rather bald assumption of superiority. Let us add to

---

(1) Gram. Lat. I. 473, as quoted by Kawczynski, p. 115.
(2) Kawczynski, p. 116.

Kawczynski's excerpt the rest of Bede's paragraph. "Metrum est ratio cum modulatione; rhythmus modulatio sine ratione; plerumque tamen casu quodam invenies etiam rationem in rhythmo non artificis moderatione servatam, sed sono et ipsa modulatione ducente, quem vulgares poetae necesse est rustice, docti faciant docte:—quomodo et ad instar iambici metri pulcherrime factus est hymnus ille praeclarus:—

> [O](1) Rex aeterne Domine,
> rerum creator omnium,
> qui eras ante saecula,
> semper cum patre filius,

et alii Ambrosiani non pauci. Item ad formam metri trochaici canunt hymnum de die judici per alphabetam;—

> Apparebit repentina
> dies magni Domini,
> fur obscura velut nocte
> improvisos occupans."(2)

Here Bede seems positively to confirm our argument. It is evident that such lines as *Rerum creator omnium*, with their apparent inversions of foot, must have been a serious puzzle to the theorists. Bede (as Kawczynki shows) borrowed most of his metrical science from the earlier grammarians, and nothing of this kind had been explained by them. Such verses were agreable enough when weighed by the "judicium aurium", but who could divide them into feet? They seemed to have no method in their irregularity. But it is evident enough from the words "*instar iambici metri*" and "*ad formam metri*

---

(1) Note that as Bede quotes the first line of this hymn its syllabic regularity is destroyed, while a certain accentual rhythm remains. MSS. vary as to the presence or absence of the interjection. Similar irregularities, by the way, are found in lines 53 and 59 of the same hymn, but they did not prevent Bede from praising it.

(2) De Arte Metrica, § 24.

trochaici" that the practical effect of these verses was to Bede's ear just what it is to us:—and he thought that the imitation of the classical iambics had been "most beautifully done". The difficulty that perplexed Bede, and drove so many of Kawczynski's authorities to deny the existence of any "modus" in these verses, was a purely theoretical one. The same difficulty is encountered in modern English verse. Theoretical investigators are not now agreed as to the essential principles which control poets of the 19th century: they do not know whether our blank verse is divisible into feet or not, nor whether it requires in each line three, four or five accents, or indeed any determinate number. If the Latin grammarians could have had revealed to them a few lines of *Paradise Lost*, they would doubtless have described it substantially as they did their own accentual verse-forms; for in both, the underlying principles of internal structure are substantially the same. Their definitions are not, therefore, to be cited as authoritative, but should be set down as due to an interesting bewilderment, which they could hardly have escaped without superhuman insight.

§ 37. *Conclusion.* It is unnecessary to follow in detail the later history of the rhythmical versification. The latest developments of the Ambrosian hymn, which we have already examined, were but the logical consequences of such work as we have found done by Fortunatus. From Ambrose himself to Adam of St. Victor, the line of descent is direct. It was doubtless in the 8 syllable iambic verse that the change from metric to rhythmic was effected; and this was done under the fostering influence of the Ambrosian music;—but how large a share of credit must be assigned to the latter, we of course cannot tell precisely. The new principle spread rapidly to other forms of verse, and at an early, though now uncertain date, hymns in trochaics began to show an equally marked accentual rhythm. The hymn "Ad perennis vitae fontem", of which a few lines have already been quoted,(1) shows what we may perhaps regard as a development from the style of verse employed by Augustine, evolved under the influence of the new idea. Mone thinks this hymn was written about a century after Augustine's time. Perhaps it would be safer to put it a little later, but we cannot be exact. It is very interesting to note that the Ambrosian hymn, which began with perfect iambic regularity, developed in the middle ages into a form so irregular as to make modern scholars call it purely syllabic; while the trochaic rhythm, which seems to correspond with the purely syllabic verse of Augustine, became almost perfectly regular when the accentual principle took possession of it. Here we have a most striking refutation of the view that historical influences are stronger than the natural conditions of language and the fitness of things.

The proof that the Ambrosian verse was governed by the accentual principle, is clinched by comparison of it with the work of its French imitators. Consideration of these latter, however, is more conveniently postponed to the next chapter. Evidence many also be found in iambic hymns other than octosyllabic. One of the earliest of these is the "Aurea luce et decore roseo", ascribed to Elpis. If this hymn was really written by the wife of Boethius, it must have been as early as the first quarter of the sixth century; but here again we have to rest in doubt. The hymn contains 28 lines of 12 syllables each, and there are only two instances of inversions other than initial.

Something has been made of the verse of the mystery play on the foolish virgins, in which the Latin verses, though so late, are plainly not accentual. Part

---

(1) § 8, *ante.*

of the verses are Latin and part French, and in both the structure is for the most part merely syllabic. It is sufficient to say of this, however, that the verses were obviously written for musical recitation, and the Latin metre was designed to correspond with the French. The bad quality of the Latin shows that French was to the author the more familiar language. It will be made clear in the next chapter that a Latin imitation of a French form of verse can prove nothing as to the nature of true Latin verse.

CHAPTER V.
Early French Verse.

§ 38. *Introduction.* It has already been intimated that the accentual rhythm of mediæval Latin poetry exhibits a fair parallel to the ordinary rhythm of modern English verse. Thus in the lines

> Ad perennis vitae fontem mens sitivit arida,

and

> Aurea luce et decore roseo,

we find the same rhythms that are so familiar in

> Comrades leave me here a little, while as yet 'tis early morn,

and

> This is my son, mine own Telemachus.

It has been seen that the licenses which the poets of the two languages have allowed themselves have been in some respects different: but their verse-forms in general have been controlled by the same essential principles. Now Latin rhythmical hymns have been familiar to English poets of every generation since the time of Bede, and it seems not unlikely that our verse would have assumed substantially its present forms, if it had had no other foreign model to imitate. In that case this investigation might fitly end here. But in point of fact our most important verse-forms, so far as they have been borrowed at all from abroad, have been borrowed from the Latin largely by an indirect process. The Latin influence was felt, during a critical period in the history of our versification, almost solely through the medium of the French. It is one of the remarkable facts in the history of the subject,—one of the facts tending most strongly to negative Kawczynski's theory of the supreme power of external influences,—that though the French system itself was widely different from the Latin, yet when it came in contact with the English it had the effect of moulding the latter into substantially the Latin form. The remaining chapters of this essay will briefly review the development of the French system out of the Latin, and its influence upon the English.

§ 39. *Modern French verse.* The essential principles of modern French versification are most clearly discernible in the Alexandrine. A fairly typical passage is subjoined, to illustrate the main features of this verse.

> Quoi, madame! parmi tant de sujets de crainte,
> Ce sont là les frayeurs dont vous êtes atteinte?
> Un cruel (comment puis-je autrement l'appeler?)
> Par la main de Calchas s'en va vous immoler;
> Et lorsqu'à sa fureur j'oppose ma tendresse,
> Le soin de son repos est le seul qui vous presse!
> On me ferme la bouche! on l'excuse, on le plaint!
> C'est pour lui que l'on tremble; et c'est moi que l'on craint!
> Triste effet de mes soins! est-ce donc là, madame,
> Tout le progrès qu'Achille avait fait dans votre âme?
> *Iphigénie* III, 6, 73—82.

Here we have verses of twelve(1) syllables each. The 6th and 12th syllables are always tonic, and there is a fixed cæsura after the 6th.(2) There is no other syl-

---

(1) The 13th syllable in the feminine rimes need not be counted, as it is not pronounced.

(2) The modern romantic forms of the Alexandrine need not concern us in the present inquiry.

lable in the verse which must be tonic, or which can be said even to be generally so; and on the other hand there is no place in the line which must be filled with an atonic syllable. The 5th and 11th are commonly atonic, but not necessarily so.

Owing to the weakness of the word-accent in French, —the fact that it tends continually to lose itself in rhetorical emphasis,—the scientific principles which underlie French versification have not been easy to discover. Even now so keen an observer as Stengel suggests(1) that such verses as those above quoted should be recognized as divisible into feet of equal length; that they move with a definite accentual rhythm, and that the frequent conflict of accent with ictus is one of the chief beauties of the form. This however is not the prevailing opinion. There is in reality no conflict of word-accent with verse-accent, because the latter, in the ordinary sense of the word, does not exist at all except at the verse-end. Of the six syllables in each hemistich, one, two, three or four may be tonic; and provided one of these is in the 6th place, the others arrange themselves in obedience to no other laws than those of euphony. It frequently happens, of course, that a French Alexandrine gives substantially the rhythm of the corresponding English verse. Thus we find this rhythm in

  Et lorsqu'à sa fureur j'oppose ma tendresse:

and such a line as

  Quoi madame! parmi tant de sujets de crainte

may with difficulty be fitted to the English scheme:— compare Spenser's

  As the God of my life? Why hath he me abhord?
             F. Q. I. 3. 7.

But this is an extreme case of the English Alexandrine,

---

(1) p. 8, § 13.

and the parallel even here is forced. Such verses moreover, as

> On me ferme la bouche! on l'excuse, on le plaint!
> C'est pour lui que l'on tremble; et c'est moi que l'on craint!

cannot be regarded as possessing any rhythm except an anapæstic one. Their rhythmic parallels in English are such lines as Byron's

> For the Angel of Death spread his wings on the blast.
> *The Destruction of Sennacherib.*

The only apparent element of regularity, then, in the internal structure of this style of versification, is the uniform number of syllables. That a Teuton like Stengel should regard the ordinary accentual reading of French poetry as destructive of its proper character, and should contend for an ideal iambic rhythm, is therefore not to be wondered at, for the Germanic ear is not satisfied without a more or less regular ictus.(1) It is true that even to the Frenchman, with his habit of approximately equalizing his stresses in ordinary speech, the rhythmical movement of French poetry is far less of a sensuous gratification than that of English poetry is to us. Its nearness to prose is a serious disadvantage,(2) and

---

(1) For example Köster (*Schiller als Dramaturg*, p. 96) regards a trochee in German blank verse, even when initial, as a violation of law, justifiable only in special cases. German poets are of course much more chary of inversions than the English.

(2) For example, " Les vers ou l'on traite des sujets familiers et simples ne sont que de la prose mesurée, ou sont obligés de s'ennoblir à l'aide de la périphrase et de l'emploi du mot *noble* en place du mot propre "—G. Paris, *L'Accent Latin*, 125. The comparatively low value of mere syllabism, from an æsthetic point of view, is well illustrated by a recent incident of French criticism. " The French Academy has the bestowal of a prize,—le prix Archon-Despérouses,—for the 'most notable volume of verse during the year'. This year the prize was voted to the *'Maison de l'Enfance'* by M. Gregh. But after the decision a horrible discovery was made. Some of M. Gregh's Alexandrines had thirteen or even fourteen syllables:—some lacked the regular cæsura; some were loosely rhymed.

for the elements of supreme beauty the French poet has to resort to other devices than those of rhythm.

As compared with English or German verse, then, that of the French poets is almost purely syllabic. Praiseworthy efforts have been made(1) to analyze it by feet, and the laws governing the various verse-forms have been ascertained by forcible and (as it seems) sound reasoning. But these laws are in reality the laws partly of chance and partly of euphony,—not strictly speaking the laws of French poetry. French verse, to adapt the description of Bede, "est verborum modulatio non *rhythmica* ratione, sed numero syllabarum ad judicium aurium examinata": and the question what will and what will not satisfy the "judicium aurium" is in a sense a general one, belonging to the whole study of æsthetics rather than to French versification in particular.

The structure of other forms of French verse is the same in principle as that of the Alexandrine. Without considering details it will suffice to point out that all forms are, in general, syllabic and not rhythmical. Thus the sonnet of Alfred de Musset's beginning *J'ai perdu ma force et ma vie* is written throughout in octosyllabics;—but it contains lines which could not be matched, as to accentual rhythm, by lines from any one English poem. For example, the line

> Dieu parle, il faut qu'on lui réponde

is like

> On Linden when the sun was low:

and

> Ici bas ont tout ignoré

The poems might be interesting, but how could Academicians overlook their irregularities? They finally compromised by adopting a minute which practically said, 'As poets we approve of M. Gregh, as Academicians we condemn him". *N.-Y. Evening Post,* June 7, 1897, p. 6.

(1) Notably by *Lubarsch.*

may be matched by a line from Tennyson's *"In the Garden at Swainston"*
> With a love that ever will be.

But the latter poem contains no eight-syllable iambic verses, and *Hohenlinden* contains no verse like the last quoted: while in the French poem the two lines given above, though so different in rhythm, are used and regarded as equivalent.

The same is of course true of the 10-syllable verse, — the only other form which we need consider. The beginning of Béranger's beautiful *Chant du Cosaque* illustrates the ordinary form of this verse.

> Viens, mon coursier, noble ami du Cosaque,
> Vole au signal des trompettes du Nord.
> Prompt au pillage, intrépide a l'attaque,
> Prête sous moi des ailes à la Mort.

In this, as in the Alexandrine, there is a fixed cæsura. The verse thus resolves itself into hemistichs of 4 and 6 syllables respectively. But these hemistichs, with the exception that the last effective syllable must be tonic, are purely syllabic. Thus while the 4th line of the extract seems like a line of English heroic verse with the ordinary initial inversion, the 2d line corresponds rather with our 4-accent verse. Such lines as

> Beat to the noiseless music of the night!

and

> That a calamity hard to be borne?

(both from *Maud*), though each contains just 10 syllables, are ordinarily, of course, felt in English to have very different rhythms.

§ 40. *The origin of French versification.* The discussion as to the origin of French versification has chiefly centred about the decasyllabic verse. This has been variously derived from the Phalæcian, the Sapphic, the iambic trimeter, the trimeter scazon, the dactylic hexameter, the dactylic trimeter hypercatalectic, and the Old High German long line of four accents. Finally Stengel derives it from a hypothetical popular Latin verse of 14 syllables, which in turn was directly descended from the Saturnian;—thus assuming a continuous stream of verse, 13 centuries long, all of which is lost.(1)

In criticism of this varied assortment of supposed explanations there is little to add to the excellent remarks of G. Paris.(2) "Avant d'essayer de montrer comment s'est constitué la système de la versification française, il faut étudier comment s'est établi, à l'époque antérieure, le principe de la versification rhythmique en regard de la versification métrique. Une fois ce principe constitué, les différents vers en sont naturellement issus, sans que chacun d'eux ait un rapport direct avec une des formes de la versification métrique, d'origine grecque, devenues toutes, pour le peuple, incompréhensibles avec le principe même de cette versification."

This seems to assume that the mediæval Latin rhythms, like the modern French, were not accentual; that the two systems are fundamentally the same, and that therefore, when the origin of the former is found, the origin of the latter is found along with it.(3) Now we have already seen that the Latin rhythms *were*

---

(1) See Stengel, pp. 14—20 for this derivation, and for the bibliography of most of the others. Substantially the same theory as Stengel's was proposed as early as 1844 for the Italian hendecasyllabic by L. G. Blanc, Gramm. der Ital. Spr. p. 706.

(2) *Romania* XV, 138 (Quoted also by Stengel).

(3) It is especially easy for a Frenchman to overlook the accentual character of the Latin rhythms, as the important part played in them by the secondary accents of Latin words can hardly appeal strongly to his ear. I trust it does not seem arrogant to admit a certain preference for the judgment of our English senses in these matters. Our own training happens to be better adapted to the purpose than that of either the French or the Germans.

accentual:—but it is also true that the earliest French verses were accentual also, and the substance of M. Paris's remark is therefore still good. We shall find that the French versification in its earliest form was a mere imitation of the Latin rhythmic system, as the latter has been explained in the foregoing pages. The change to the system now prevailing in French took place after the period of this imitation was past, and was presumably due to causes inherent in the language itself. Our search, in obedience to M. Paris's precept, should be for general principles rather than for single parallels:—but as it happens we shall find that the familiar verse of the Ambrosian hymns, and its French offspring, exhibit the true principles most clearly.

§ 41. *The earliest octosyllabics.* That the *Eulalia* sequence was an accentual poem has been mentioned already, but we are not directly concerned with it now because it is unique in its peculiar style. It is important here only as indicating, perhaps, that the natural tendency of the earliest French verse-makers was toward accentual composition.

The next in order of the early monuments of French verse are the *Passion-poem* (516 lines) and the *Life of St. Léger* (240 lines), both of the 10th century, and the Fragment of the *Alexander Romance* ascribed to Alberic of Besançon (105 lines), which dates probably from the first half of the 11th century. All these poems are in 8-syllable lines, and the rhythm of all is unquestionably accentual, with a marked iambic movement.(1) A few lines from the first-named poem will make this clear.(2)

---

(1) This was first pointed out, I think, by G. Paris, in his remarks on the *St. Léger*, in *Romania* I, 295; but its significance does not seem to have been duly appreciated.

(2) I take these from the beginning of the excerpt given in Bartsch's *Chrestomathie*, which is probably the text most easily accessible.

117. Christus Jhesus den s'en leved,
Gehsemani vil' es n'anez.
Toz sos fidels seder rovet,
Avan orar sols en anet.

121. Granz fu li dols, fort marrimenz.
Si condormirent tuit ades.
Jhesus cum veg los esveled,
trestoz orar ben los manded.

Here the rhythm is an obvious reproduction of that of the Ambrosian hymns, even the division into four-verse strophes being retained. There are frequent inversions,— as in the first foot of the 121st line,—but the general iambic movement is unmistakable.

Indeed the iambic movement seems more marked than it does in the Latin hymns, because of the fact that initial inversions are generally only single, not double. Thus a tonic syllable is almost always found in the 4th place. The verse is thus characteristically distinguished from that of modern French, and in this respect it differs slightly even from that of the Latin hymns.

The degree of regularity with which the 4th syllable was made tonic is worth noting. Of the 100 lines of the *Passion* which include and follow the above excerpt, there are 73 with a final tonic syllable in the 4th place (e. g. *Toz sos fidels*), and 25 with a penultimate tonic syllable there (*Si condormirent*).(1) The other two lines have each a final syllable at the fourth place, but that syllable is atonic. These lines are

Melz ti fura(2) non fusses naz (151)

---

(1) I have separated these two types of verse, lest the figures should seem to suggest that the early octosyllabic had a fixed cæsura. This has sometimes been fancied, but is obviously not true.

(2) It is barely possible that in these pluperfects the accent was thrown forward, contrary to the general principles of O. F. etymology. If so the line is regular. In l. 168 we have Quar sua fin veder voldrat, where the assonance and syllabic structure both show that voldrat must be oxy-

and

Mult lez semper en esdevint (210).

Here of course the exceptions are so few that they do not even threaten the rule. In the poem on St. Léger the verse is substantially the same. Of the first 100 lines, 81 have a tonic final syllable in the fourth place, 13 a tonic syllable not final, and 6 a final atonic syllable. These last are the following:—

Que il auuret ab duos seniors	(8)
Quandius visquet ciel reis Lothier	(49)
Il lo presdrent tuit a conseil	(61)
A nuil omne nol demonstrat	(78)
Quant ciel ire tels esdevint(1)	(79)
Paschas furent in eps cel di	(80)

In the Alexander fragment there are 73 lines with a tonic final syllable in the fourth place, 26 with a tonic syllable not final, 4 with a final syllable not tonic, and 2 with a syllable neither final nor tonic.(2) The lines belonging to these last two classes are as follows:—

En tal forma fud naz lo reys	(54)
Que altre emfes de quatro meys	(57)
Que altre emfes del seyentreyr	(75)
A fol omen ne ad escueyr	(78)

and

Toylle sen otiositas	(6)
Ne ad emperadur servir	(43)

---

tonic;—but I should prefer to regard this as an instance of wrenched accent. Cf. l. 134, *Zo lor demandent que querent*, where the wrenched accent is obvious.

(1) A doubtful reading: but no plausible emendation normalizes the verse. In one line of this passage, viz (18) *rovat que litteras apresist*, we must either read *letres*, with G. Paris, or assume a syncope in the Latin word *litteras*.

(2) Although G. Paris says (*Romania* I, 296): " Dans l'Alexandre l'accentuation de la troisième syllable, reste de la rhythmopoée latine, a tout-a-fait disparu: le vers est toujours divisé en deux moitiés egales, accentués pareillement sur la dernière ". This I do not at all understand.

One of these last two lines, and perhaps both, may be regarded as regular if we recognize the principle of secondary accent:—but it is safer to class them as exceptions. Lines certainly do occur with the 4th syllable neither tonic nor final; e. g. in the *Passion*,

  Barrabant perdonent la vide (225).

 § 42. *The later development of French octosyllabics.* After the middle of the 11th century, this ceased to be the regular style of French versification. Examples do occur in which the adherence to the accentual movement is more or less rigid, but they are from Anglo-Norman poems, or from the work of poets exposed to the Anglo-Norman influence, and they are easily explained as due to the retroactive influence of English versification. In pure French octosyllabics, the modern system asserted itself early. This fact is of such importance in the history of English verse that it deserves more detailed consideration.

 Schipper says:(1) "In der mittelalterlich-lateinischen Poesie, sowie auch in der romanischen, ist... eine regelmässige Aufeinanderfolge von stärker und schwächer betonten Silben oder von Hebungen und Senkungen Gesetz, die beide von gleichem Wert für den Rhythmus sind". And again, speaking of French octosyllabics, he says: "Zwei Verspaare aus dem Roman de Brut des Wace mögen das Wesen dieses Metrums veranschaulichen:

  Cordeille out bien escuté
  et bien out en sun cuer noté
  cument ses deus sorurs parloënt,
  cument lur pere losengoënt.

Wir haben hier ein Versmass von im Ganzen jambischen Rhythmus vor uns ".(2)

---

(1) P. 79.
(2) Id. p. 107. This is a common error. E. g. Courthope, *Hist. Eng.*

But the rhythm of Wace's poem is by no means iambic. The first word in the passage quoted forms an anapæst (and should be written with a diærisis, Cordeïlle), as is shown by its use at the verse-end eight lines before this excerpt:—

Adunt apela Cordeille

(riming with *fille*); and again 60 lines later we have

Cordeille qui fu li mendre

(riming with *atendre*). Indeed the whole passage in the original is quite as nearly anapæstic as iambic, as the ten lines before Schipper's quotation will show:—

Mult a ci | dist il | grant amur,
ne te sai | demander | graignur;
jo te redunrai | bon seignur
et la tier | ce part | de m'enur.
Adunt | apela | Cordeïlle
qui esteit | sa plus joes | ne fille;
pur ce que il | l'aveit | plus chiere
que Ragaü | ne la premiere
quida | que el | e cuneüst
que plus chier | des al | tres l'eüst.
Cordeïl | le out bien | escuté, etc.

Indeed, of the first 100 lines of the passage in Bartsch's *Chrestomathie* (from which Schipper quotes), there are only 57 with a tonic syllable in the 4th place; and most of the other 43 are clearly anapaestic.

This passage is, to be sure, rather more unfavorable to Schipper's generalization than others which he might have cited. Chrestien of Troyes, for example, exhibits

---

Poetry I, 110, says: "When through the genius of Chaucer the *French iambic movement* was naturalized in the Middle English, the triple movement, inherent in the old style, gave way before the new tendency". So also Crow, *Zur Gesch. d. Kurzen Reimpaars im M. Eng.*, p. 6, says: "Im Französischen besteht das Schema des kurzen Reimpaars aus zwei durch Endreime gebundenen Versen von je vier jambischen Füssen, meist mit Caesur nach den zweiten".

a slightly less strong tendency to the anapæstic movement. Thus in the first 100 lines of his *Chevaliers au Lion* there are some 24 that have a regular iambic rhythm throughout, as in

>   Si s'est de lez le roi levee;   (63)

and 43 more exhibit the chief characteristic form of the earliest French rhythm, namely the tonic syllable in the 4th place, as in

>   Uns cortois mors qu'uns vilains vis. (32)

But on the other hand there are at least 25 that have a markedly anapæstic movement,—i. e. two anapæstic feet and one iambus, in any one of the three possible arrangements: e. g.

>   Li autre parloient d'amors   (13)
>   Si m'acort de tant as Bretons   (37)
>   Se feisoient cortois clamer   (22)

The remaining lines are of hybrid character, and it is not worth while here to attempt an exact classification. Of course, figures of this sort cannot be relied on for absolute precision, for the scansion of many lines depends upon one's individual taste. For example, the verse

>   Et cil fable et mançonge en font   (25)

will entirely change its character according to the degree of rhetorical emphasis on *cil*. But the foregoing estimates have been kept purposely conservative: and it must be perfectly apparent that before the time of Wace or Chrestien the change in French verse had become established. Their verse, far from being "in the main iambic", was as purely syllabic as that of the 19th century.

§ 43. *The difference between Latin and Old French verse.* We shall now have to consider the reasons for such changes as we have seen in the octosyllabic metre; —first the change from Latin to Old French, and second the change from Old to Mediæval French. Stengel, while recognizing the essential facts of the history, seems to give an entirely mistaken explanation of them. He seems to regard the early specimens of French accentual verse as the last examples of a decaying school,—a remnant from popular verse-forms that have perished, not from the well-known Latin rhythms. And he says:(1) "Gewöhnte man sich in Anlehnung an den gleichsilbigen Vers der rhythmisch-lateinischen Verskunst früh daran, statt an vierter öfters an dritter Stelle einen Wortton zuzulassen (freilich anfänglich nur, wenn als vierte eine Wortschlusssilbe folgte), so wurde damit gerade das Gegenteil von dem bewirkt, was die Betonung der vierten Silbe bezweckte, der jambische Rhythmus wurde verdunkelt, und damit erschien auch jede weitere Markierung desselben im Innern des Verses überflüssig". Here it is implied that the earliest French rhythms were in their accentual character, essentially different from the Latin; and secondly we are told that the change in French rhythms was due to Latin influence. It is clear enough that both these opinions must be erroneous; but we will nevertheless examine them separately in detail.

In the first place, is it true that in the Ambrosian hymns it was a common thing to accent the third syllable at the expense of the fourth? How far, if at all, was the distinguishing characteristic of early French verse lacking in that of the Latin hymns?

For the purpose of answering these questions, a special examination has been made of the six Ambrosian hymns already used for another purpose.(2) The results may be conveniently tabulated as follows:—

---

(1) P. 46.
(2) § 27, *ante*.

First line	Total lines	Accent on 4th	Accent not on 4th
Jesu nostra redemptio	20	18	2
Hymnum dicamus Domino	32	26	6
Christe qui lux es et dies	24	23	1
Aurora lucis rutilat	44	38	6
O rex aeterne Domine	64	57	7
Mediae noctis tempus est	52	42	10
Total:	236	204	32

The lines tabulated as having an accent on the 4th syllable are of course either regular iambic lines, such as

Ut ferres nostra crimina,

or lines with a single initial inversion, such as

Amor et desiderium.

The right-hand column in the table includes all lines with double inversion, such as the title line of the first hymn.

The table shows that on an average about six-sevenths of the lines in an ordinary Ambrosian hymn are accented on the 4th syllable. In the three passages of the earliest French verse already examined, the total ratio is about nineteen-twentieths. In other words, the proportion of comparatively regular lines is 11 per cent larger in Old French than in Latin.

§ 44. *Explanation of the difference.* This numerical discrepancy does not seem sufficient to count for much against the judgment of our ears as to the substantial identity of the two rhythms; but in order to eliminate the element of personal judgment it will be well to show that the discrepancy is in fact of just the sort that we ought to expect.

In the first place, it must be remembered that some of the Latin verses which we have counted in the last column of the table, must probably have been brought into conformity with the regular type by reading with wrenched accents. In such a passage as the following, from *Aurora lucis rutilat,*

> Tristes erat apostoli
> de nece sui Domini,
> quem poena mortis crudeli
> servi damnarunt impii,

it is certain that *crudeli* must have been read as a proparoxytone, although, as has already been shown, it is an extreme example of the wrenched accent. It therefore seems very likely that such lines as

> Fellaces Judaeii impii,

and

> Laudes Deo cum cantico,

(both from the *Hymnum dicamus*) were read with a similar license in the placing of the second accent. This is especially probable in the case of dissyllabic proper names, which are well known to have been treated with great freedom. Now in French this license was comparatively impracticable. The Latin poets wrote in a language that was nearly or quite dead to vulgar conversational use, and it is probable that they pronounced it in a measured manner, each syllable receiving its due value,(1) so that with the tradition of quantitative verse

---

(1) The exact proportion of wrenched accents to inversions of foot, in the Ambròsian hymns, is so uncertain that I have not cared to enforce this branch of the argument as any thing more than a suggestion. The main reason, however, for my conjecture as to the pronunciation of Latin may be explained by reference to the treatment of rime in Latin and French, as compared with English. In modern French, identical rime (under the name of *rime riche*) is often desired: in English it is usually intolerable. The chief reason for this seems to be that the tonic accent is weak in French,—in English comparatively strong. Thus such a French rime as *tombé, malgré,* is almost like the English half-rime *candle, pestle.* The latter is improved by substituting *cradle* for *pestle*; still more, perhaps, by *bundle*: and so in French the poet in many cases seeks identity of con-

behind them it was a small matter to throw forward the accent of a dissyllable. But the French poet had no such traditions to influence him in his use of the vernacular, and he used a language in which, while enunciation in general may possibly have been as measured as it is now, the final unaccented syllables are known to have been grievously scanted.(1) While therefore he could in Latin say *homó*, he could not so well say, in French, *omné*. If, therefore, we could fix the percentage of lines in the Ambrosian hymns which were actually normalized by throwing an accent forward, we could fairly deduct this percentage from the difference which we have to account for, since it would stand for a type which the Frenchman, in the nature of things, could not imitate.(2)

In the second place, disregarding the possibility of occasional wrenched accents, if we read the Latin hymns accentually throughout, we find in them many inversions such as the French poet would not be tempted to indulge in. The greater number of the lines in the hymns which (under such an accentual reading) do not accent the 4th syllable, have their second feet filled by dissyllables. E. g. in the *Hymnum dicamus* we find the following:

    Laudes Deo cum cantico,   (2)
    Qui nos crucis patibulo,   (3)
    Nullam culpam invenio,   (22)
    Vita mundi suspenditur: (31)

---

sonants before the riming vowel. A similar fondness for identical rime in the Latin hymns seems to me explicable only on the hypothesis of a similar weakness of the tonic accent in the half-artificial pronunciation of late Latin.

(1) This, I suppose, will not be doubted. It is shown (1) by the curious variety in the spelling of these syllables, and their phonetic changes in general, and (2) by their subsequent disappearance from ordinary speech.

(2) Wrenched accents are found in the Old French poems, as for example in the line cited *ante*, § 41, *note*; but they are rare.

and it is evident that this rhythm must result whenever the poet's convenience led him to begin a verse with two dissyllables. But when a French poet chose to do the same thing, he would find in most cases that the rhythm adjusted itself to the normal scheme, for most of the dissyllabic words in his vocabulary were oxytonic.(1)

A third fact, tending further to explain why inversions are less frequent in the first French poems than in their Latin models, is perhaps less obvious. When, in a line in an Ambrosian hymn, the 4th syllable is not accented, the accent is almost always found on the 3rd;—and in these cases, again, another accent is almost always found on the 1st:—in other words, a simple case of double inversion is presented. Now such a verse as

Laudes Deo cum cantico,

read strictly according to the word-accent, gives an agreeable rhythm which to an English ear does not seriously disturb the general iambic movement of the hymn;—just as the general iambic movement of *Paradise Lost* is not disturbed by the double inversion in such a passage as

There with my cries importune Heaven, that all
The sentence, from thy head removed, may light
On me, sole cause to thee of all this woe,
Me, me only, just object of His ire.
X, 933—936.

But in a French verse in which the 3rd syllable was accented, it was less easy to put another accent on the 1st. Such a verse might begin with a word of 1, 2, 3 or 4 syllables. In either of the last two cases the first syllable of the line could not be heavily enough accented to save the rhythm, for if the secondary accent existed at all in the Old French it was certainly pretty weak.

---

(1) See, for example, the passage quoted from the Passion poem, §41, *ante*, in which the sixteen dissyllables are all oxytones.

In consequence, the verse would begin with a marked anapæstic movement, and the homogeneity of the rhythm would be at once imperiled. Moreover, if the line began with a dissyllable, the same result would generally follow, unless the dissyllable was one of the comparatively infrequent variety with accent on the penult:—for otherwise, according to a principle familiar to students of modern French versification, the accent of the first word would usually be lost in the collision with that of the second.(1)

Reference back to the several lines quoted as exceptional from the oldest French poems will show that when the 3rd syllable was accented instead of the 4th, initial dissyllables were apparently not desired (unless, of course, they were paroxytones), and initial polysyllables were carefully avoided. In other words, the poet generally sought those few combinations of words which would secure an accent on the 1st syllable also: but the effect, so far as we can judge, was not always successful. In

> Melz ti fura non fusses naz

there is a strong rhetorical stress on the first monosyllable, and the effect is as good as that of

> Paschas furent in eps cel di;

but in such lines as

> Il lo presdrent tuit a conseil

there seems to be a real change to an anapæstic movement,—the same that we found in Alfred de Musset's

> Ici bas ont tout ignoré

---

(1) See Lubarsch, p. 40 *et seq*. This principle of modern verse is due largely to the general weakness and mobility of French accents. This branch of the argument, therefore, loses part of its force if it can be shown that accent was very much stronger in Old French. That it was somewhat stronger, I have no doubt.

and in Wace's
> Cordeïlle out bien escuté.

Since, therefore, any departure from the system of accenting the 4th syllable was likely to result in an anapaestic movement, and so to disturb the general run of the verse, a French poet with the ideal iambic rhythm in his head would naturally be comparatively slavish in his fidelity to the strict scheme.

Finally there remains one fact which may perhaps go farther than anything else to explain the regularity of these French poems. Their authors were not poets at all. The *Passion* and the *Life of St. Léger* reveal an impressive religious earnestness,—with a good deal of the sincerest kind of mediæval asceticism,—but of artistic genius there are no traces in any of the three poems. Now regularity in rhythm is just what the poorest artist is likely to attain. He cannot make his lines smooth or sweet or majestic, but he can and generally does make his accents follow one another with mechanical regularity. These writers, it seems, were able to do this, and not much more. Where inversions do occur in their verse, they were probably introduced less for the sake of giving grace or variety to the rhythm, than because the author lacked the patience or the skill to avoid them. His ideal was more mechanical than his model, and he pursued the former except where he was obliged to resort to such licenses as the latter plainly allowed.(1)

---

(1) I have in the last few pages selected for detailed discussion only the one difference between Latin and O. F. octosyllabics which seemed to me most likely to mislead. There are two other striking differences of detail, namely the comparative frequency of inversions in the 3rd foot in French, and the use of mere assonance in the latter language after rime had been well developed in Latin. Both these phenomena can, I think, be easily explained by comparison of the exigencies of the two languages, but it did not seem worth while to swell these pages with such matters. The fact that the French verse was borrowed from the Latin seems so

§ 45. *Explanation of the change in French verse.*
This brings us to the second branch of the assertion quoted from Stengel.(1) He believes that after the time of these early poems, Frenchmen learned, by imitation of the Latin rhythms, to avoid the regular iambic movement, and to write the almost purely syllabic verse that is so familiar now. This involves a curious misconception as to the way in which the Latin influence worked. The poems in which the modern syllabic system begins to appear are for the most part romances and songs of chivalry. (This is strictly true of the 8-syllable line, although the *Alexis*, in decasyllabics, while in the main unaccentual, is anything but chivalric in feeling.) Now it is impossible to believe that the monks of the 10th century, whose business it was to study and expound Latin, should persistently adhere to a system inherited from poets of France now forgotten,—a system peculiar to the vernacular; and that the trouvères of the 11th and 12th centuries should be the ones to adopt the system of the Latin sacred song! We have seen, however, that the Latin rhythms were not, in general, purely syllabic; and it will be easy to find an explanation of the change in French verse that will be unobjectionable.

The explanation is found in the laws of French accent. Every French word is accented, (so far as its accent is fixed at all), either on the last syllable, or, in the case of feminine endings, on the penult. In the latter case the final syllable is so insignificant that the word is almost always virtually oxytonic:—and this oxytonic character is absolute in the prose of ordinary speech, and becomes absolute in poetry wherever elision occurs. If, therefore, the French write strictly accentual rhythms, their verses will of necessity show a general

---

patent, that I fear too much space has already been given in the text to unnecessary demonstration.

(1) § 43, *ante*.

identity of word-foot with verse-foot; and it is well understood that such identity is far from pleasing in its effect. It was avoided in quantitative verse by both the Greeks and the Romans, and it is avoided in accentual verse by modern poets generally. This fact has led to the great preference that the English have shown for iambic and anapæstic metres, as compared with trochaic and dactylic;—for oxytonic words in English are in a small minority. In Spanish on the other hand, it is said that trochaic rhythms are generally the favorites, and in Spanish we find a comparatively large number of oxytonic words.

The French poet who attempted to write iambic verse, quickly (though doubtless unconsciously) discovered this fact. His verses acquired that choppy character which is so annoying, for example, in *Hiawatha*; though the illustration is by no means adequate, for the tendency to throw accents back in English is far less marked than the tendency to throw them forward in French. Moreover at an early date (though perhaps we cannot say how early) the secondary accent was lost to the French language. The poet could not, therefore, make two proper metrical stresses rest upon a single word. Polysyllabic words were a source of serious embarrassment to him. Trisyllables, for example, with masculine endings, constitute anapæsts, and they would have to be ruled out of the poet's vocabulary altogether, unless the first syllable could be worked in as the last part of an inverted foot. Longer words would in general be quite impracticable:—they would sink the rhythm beyond recognition.

Thus accentual verse became an artistic impossibility.(1) As quantitative verse was equally out of the

---

(1) It has been attempted in modern French, but only experimentally, it seems, or for use with music. Lubarsch, p. 198, *et seq.*

question, it is plain that the system actually adopted, whether we regard it as satisfactory or not, was the only one available. To the modern French language it is peculiarly suited, on account of the generally equal value of syllables in the modern speech, and the lightness of the French tonic stress. How far these characteristics had been developed in the French of the middle ages, the writer has been unable to determine;(1) but it seems not unlikely that they were then present to some extent, and materially aided the introduction of the new system of verse. Stengel's theory as to the manner of its introduction is probably correct, if we disregard his explanation of the cause. " Gewöhnte man sich (*not*, however, "in Anlehnung an den gleichsilbigen Vers der rhythmisch-lateinischen Verskunst") früh daran, statt an vierter öfters an dritter Stelle einen Wortton zuzulassen ... so wurde ... der jambische Rhythmus verdunkelt, und damit erschien auch jede weitere Markierung desselben im Innern des Verses überflüssig." The irregular lines in *The Passion* and the *Life of St. Léger* look as if they were introduced merely for convenience; but those in the *Alexander* may well have been consciously written as tentative efforts at the new system: the latter seems to be the case in *Gormund et Isembard,* and after that the sway of the new system was undisputed except where foreign influence came to disturb it.

It is possible, however, that the idea of writing syllabic verse instead of accentual was suggested by a mispronunciation of Latin. Latin is now commonly pronounced by Frenchmen according to the laws of French accent,—i. e. with the accent thrown forward in all

---

(1) I should conjecture that the equal measurement of syllables was to some extent characteristic of the tongue from the first, because of the way in which the syllables *before* the accent were preserved, in the passage from low Latin to French, while those *after* the accent melted away. That, on the other hand, the Old French accent was somewhat stronger

words.(1) In the middle ages the usage in this respect seems to have been variable.(2) Thus the following lines seem to accent all the proper names on the ultimate:—

> Et *Troillus* et *Eneas*,
> roi *Menon* et *Pollidamas*,
> rois *Sarpedon* et rois *Glaucus*
> et de *Lancoine Eufrenus*, ...
> rois *Terepex*, rois *Adrastus*
> rois *Epistrox*, roi *Alcanus*, etc.
> Beneoit, *Roman de Troies* 9717, et seq.

while in the *Alexander* we have apparently the true Latin accents (including the secondary) in

> *Est vanitatum vanitas*
> *et universa vanitas.*

In the *Passion* we have, on the one hand

> Post que deus filz *suspensus* fure,

and, on the other hand,

> Jhesum querem *Nazarenum.*

Now it is easy to see that a little indulgence of this tendency to throw the accent forward would convert the accentual verse of an Ambrosian hymn into a measure purely syllabic, and the supposition that some such process gave the French poet his first suggestion is at least not violent.

To the present writer, however, it does not seem necessary to go abroad for an explanation. Here, as elsewhere, it is surely not unreasonable to repose some confidence in native genius. We have seen the necessity and propriety of the system:—we may well believe that the poets found it out for themselves.

---

than the modern, seems probable from the accentual habit of speech observed among the peasant classes, and from stage tradition.

(1) G. Paris, *Accent Latin*, p. 22, 23.

(2) M. Paris thinks we can fix the time at which the correct pronunciation of Latin passed out of use, but I am unable to follow his reasoning.

§ 46. *French decasyllabics.* Mention has already been made of the great number of derivations proposed for the 10-syllable verse in French. The excellent precept of M. Paris, however, which has been quoted, directs us to the most straightforward explanation. This verse is probably not an exotic at all, but a natural development from the principles established in the 8-syllable line. There are three difficulties in the way of this common-sense derivation which will be briefly considered:—first, the fact that in the earliest known decasyllabics the syllabic system appears firmly established,—second, that there is a fixed cæsura, usually after the fourth syllable,—and third, that there is often, in the earliest specimens, an extra-metrical syllable at the cæsura, or in other words, that the first hemistich often has a feminine ending.

The first fact occasions no surprise in view of the date of the appearance of this verse. It is first found in French in the *Life of St. Alexis,*—a poem more recent than the *Alexander* or perhaps even *Gormund et Isembard,* but older than any of the other romances. It would not have been strange, indeed, if the new system had appeared in decasyllabics long before it was established in the 8-syllable verse;—for the more syllables there were in a line, the more obvious were the disadvantages of the accentual system; but in fact the *Alexis* was written just as the new system was introduced in octosyllabics.

The second difficulty is no more serious. Given the syllabic system, long lines without cæsura were impracticable.(1) A little consideration of the possible varieties of such lines will make this clear. If we count

---

(1) They have been written, of course, by the poets of the Romantic School in the 19th century.

only those lines which could be made by combinations of iambic and anapæstic feet, we find that the following varieties might occur:

```
⏑⏑−   ⏑⏑−   ⏑−    ⏑−
⏑⏑−   ⏑−    ⏑⏑−   ⏑−
⏑⏑−   ⏑−    ⏑−    ⏑⏑−
⏑−    ⏑⏑−   ⏑⏑−   ⏑−
⏑−    ⏑⏑−   ⏑−    ⏑⏑−
⏑−    ⏑−    ⏑⏑−   ⏑⏑−
```

But the introduction of a cæsura after the 4th syllable necessarily eliminates all except the 6th of these varieties, because that is the only one that permits a tonic syllable in the 4th place. The above, now, are only the combinations of two particular kinds of feet. It is easy to see that, with the variety of other possible combinations, the condition of decasyllabics without cæsura would have been chaotic: the fixed pause was necessary to reduce the line even to such regularity as is desirable in French verse. 10 syllables arranged helter-skelter could not be counted by the ear, and the essential principle of the verse would therefore be obscured;—but 10 syllables arranged in groups of 4 and 6 are comparatively easy to grasp.

Substantially the same explanation may be given, perhaps more clearly, in another form. The French poet, we will say, was sensitive enough to feel that long verses were objectionable, in that the number of their syllables could not readily be grasped;—and therefore he did not compose long verses at all: but he found a beauty in the combination of short verses of unequal lengths. The French decasyllabic line can with entire propriety be regarded as made up of two verses, one of 4 and one of 6 syllables. The reason why it is not so regarded is that rime is not found at the cæsura, and rime is commonly insisted upon as the indispensable mark of the verse-end in French. It is of course true that French poetry in general needs rime to mark off one verse from another:—syllabic regularity alone is not enough to distinguish verse from prose: French blank verse is not verse at all. But it is clear that the longer the verse is, the more necessary does rime become, and conversely, alternate lines of 4 syllables might well be left unrimed. There is therefore no logical impropriety in regarding the 10 syllable long line as made up of two verses. Whether it should now be so regarded, is a purely academical question, but that it came into being as such seems extremely probable. The early French version of the *Song of Songs* tends strongly to confirm this opinion, for it is made up of rimed 10 syllable lines intermixed with unrimed lines of 4 syllables. The first 6 lines illustrate its verse:—

> Quant li solleiz convisct en leon
> en icel tens qu'est ortus pliadon
>   perunt matin,
> une pulcellet odit molt gent plorer
> et son ami dolcement regreter,
>   e si lli dis.

The effect of this is obviously that of a series of short verses, those of 4 syllables unrimed, those of 6 rimed. It differs from the ordinary decasyllabic only in this respect, that here the number of short verses exceeds that of the long, instead of being exactly equal. A regular alternation of unrimed 4-syllable lines with rimed 6-syllable lines, would differ from decasyllabics only in the manner of writing; and in a manuscript in which poetry is written as prose even this difference would disappear.

 The same consideration explains the third difficulty, namely the occasional presence of an extra syllable at the end of the first hemistich; for if that hemistich was understood as a separate verse, it might, of course, have either a masculine or a feminine ending. Masculine endings were the rule in the first three specimens of

French poetry(1)—as was indeed natural, since they were copied from a Latin verse in which the ending was uniformly masculine. The feminine verse-end first appears, as a regular form, in the *Alexis* itself; and that is therefore exactly the poem in which we should expect to find the extra syllable at the caesura. The new ending being once devised, it was naturally applied to the short and the long hemistichs alike.(2)

---

(1) Isolated examples of the feminine ending are found, as in ll. 127, 128 of the *Passion*.

(2) The argument is strengthened by the appearance in French of two other forms of the decasyllabic line—those, namely, with cæsura after the 5th or after the 6th syllable. They are simply other combinations of shorter metres. The efforts to find a separate classical original for each of the three are painfully superfluous. The only serious difficulty that confronts our theory is in the comparison of the decasyllabics of other romance languages. The Italian *endecasillabo*, however, is probably not a proper subject of comparison. It has no fixed cæsura, and while it has, in a sense, two fixed accents, one of these may fall either on the 4th or on the 6th syllable. While therefore it looks like a combination of two forms of the French line, and as such perhaps threatens our derivation of the latter, it is simpler to regard it as not a composite line at all, but a natural extension of the octosyllabic form. The Provençal poem *Boethius* is peculiar. Here the 1st hemistich of the decasyllable is frequently feminine, but the verse-end proper is uniformly masculine; and the structure of the verse is syllabic rather than accentual. Bartsch (*Gesch. d. Prov. Lit.* § 8) seems to think this poem was written in the 1st half of the 10th century: Stimming (in Gröber's *Grundriss*, II. 2, 44) simply says it dates from the 2nd half of the 10th century, or according to others from the beginning of the 11th. If the earliest of these dates is correct, then the poem presents an entirely isolated phenomenon, which I am at present unable to explain by my own theory, or by any other: but if the latest date is to be trusted, then the poem, while singular, need not puzzle us. I am the more content, for the present, to leave this branch of the problem partly unsolved, because the whole subject of French decasyllabic verse is only collaterally involved in our inquiry (as will appear in the next chapter).

CHAPTER VI.
Latin and French Influence in English Verse.

§ 47. *Old English verse.* Old English versification was dependent chiefly upon accent, but also in part upon quantity. The typical verse was composed of two hemistichs. The normal hemistich may perhaps most logically be analyzed as composed of four measures. Two of these measures were accented, and consisted in general of single long syllables; but sometimes an accented measure comprised (by a species of resolution) two short syllables, of which the first received the actual stress; and in a special class of cases an accented measure might even consist of a single short syllable. The other two measures in each hemistich were unaccented (either actually or comparatively) and each consisted, generally speaking, of an indeterminate number of syllables, indifferently short or long. The regular accents of the hemistich might fall upon any two of the four measures, except only that one, at least, of the accents must fall upon one of the first two measures. Alliteration bound together the two hemistichs of each verse.(1)

Such was the structure of the simplest verses,—the five types announced by Sievers; but complications were common. Without considering the latter, however, we necessarily feel that the rhythm of the verse was hardly

---

(1) This description is taken from Sievers, p. 23 *et seq.*, with changes only in the form of statement.

a rhythm at all, in any modern sense. However studiously we accustom our ears to it, there seems still to be a barbaric crudeness inherent in the verse:—and yet the investigations of Sievers have revealed complex laws such as could have been evolved only in a refined form of art. It is evident therefore that while we understand the laws of composition in minute detail, we have not yet perfectly realized the actual manner and effect of the customary recitation of the lines.(1) Perhaps they were delivered in a musical or quasi-musical manner, and in this recitative the time may have been quite as salient a feature as the stress; so that occasional pauses might effect an approximate equality between the measures:— but the details are yet to be established. Certainly the verse-form was well grounded in the character of the language: it changed as the language changed, and some such mode of recitation as we have suggested can probably be proved by examination of the curious phases of decay through which the verse passed,—betraying hopeless efforts to shape the new materials into the old form. That inquiry, however, is not within our present province.

§ 48. *The decay of Old English Verse.* This verse fell into decay in two ways.(2) The more conservative poets of the early middle ages probably reproduced the effect of it as well as they knew how. Their verses and those of their followers reveal a loss of the more refined feeling for quantity, a loss of the peculiar Old English distinction of half-accents, and often a tendency to fill up the unstressed measures with multitudes of syllables; but the real continuity of the verse-form is apparent even down to our own time. We trace it in its decay

---

(1) The necessity of further study of this subject is made clear by Heath, *Trans. Phil. Soc.* 1891—93, p. 375.

(2) Schipper, p. 76 and *passim.*

to the doggerel verse found so frequently in the morality plays, and even in Shakspere's early comedies; rarer examples are to be found in the 17th and 18th centuries; and the 19th has resuscitated and beautifully refined such of its essential principles as had any life in them, in the familiar Christabel metre. A large part of our modern verse has thus descended directly from the Old English long line. It counts not the number of syllables, but the number of accents, and it owes nothing, *in principle,* to foreign influence, except the principle of rime.(1) We are therefore not concerned with it here.

The other main line of descent from the Old English verse has a modern representative, too; but this line is a devious one, and is not unbroken. It is here, chiefly, that Schipper shows the direct interference of foreign influences. Following this line down from the earliest times, we find at the beginning of the 12th century the first marked divergence from the conservative course just outlined. This divergence occurred when the long line was embellished with leonine rime,—an ornament imported, of course, from the continent.(2) The result was virtually to turn the hemistichs into separate verses, and to oust alliteration, at least as an essential element of the verse. Next we find that the short lines thus formed, by virtue of the tendency to multiplication of syllables already mentioned, are by no means limited to two accents, but commonly take three or even four.(3) With deference, however, to the views of Schipper (and others quoted by him), it must be insisted that the third and fourth accents in these early verses are not essential

---

(1) Of course it would not have attained its present smooth perfection if our poets had not in the meantime trained their ears in the practice of other forms of verse, under foreign tutelage.

(2) Schipper, 146 *et seq.* This device was used, of course, at an earlier date; but its effect first becomes fully apparent in Layamon's *Brut.*

(3) Schipper, 180, *et seq.*

features of the rhythm. In such a passage as the following, for example,

> Hi wénden to wísse
> Of here líf to mísse.
> Al the dáy and al the níght
> Til hit spráng day líght,
> *King Horn*, 121—4.

it is clear that if we regard the first verse as having two essential accents, the second three, and the third four, the rhythm ceases at once to be homogeneous. We should read such a passage with especial regard to the two principle stresses in each line;—they are the ones that determine the rhythm;—and the subsidiary stresses will then be found to cause no disturbance. The true character of this rhythm can best be realized by comparing it with a modern imitation, like Lamb's "*Old Familiar Faces*". In this, each verse has its four accents, two in each hemistich; and the other accents that occasionally intrude are to be regarded as unessential. Compare the stanza already quoted(1) with the following:

> How sóme they have díed, and sóme they have léft me,
> And sóme are taken fróm me; áll are depárted;
> All, all are góne, the óld familiar fáces.

§ 49. *Development of English verse under foreign influence*. Before the date of *King Horn*, new ideas of versification had been introduced into English poetry from abroad. The *Poema Morale* and the *Pater-noster* exhibit verse-forms that are based upon the number of accents, to be sure, like the strictly English forms already considered; but the number of accents is a new one. The verse of the *Poema Morale* has seven, that of the *Pater-noster* four. Examples will make this structure clear.

---

(1) In § 4, *ante*.

Se man that wille siker bien to habbe godes blisce,
Do evre god, ther hwile he mai; thanne haveth he hit to iwisse:
Tho riche weneth siker bien thurgh walles and thurgh diches;
Se deth his heghte on sikere stede, that sent hi to hevenriche.
Poema Morale 19-24.

>Ure feder thet in heovene is,
>That is al soth ful iwis!
>Weo moten to theos weordes iseon,
>Thet to live and to saule gode beon.
>
>*Pater-noster*, 1-4.

For the metre of the first of these two poems Schipper easily shows a Latin origin.(1) The imitation is unmistakable. But as to the second he falls into the error of deriving it from the Old French octosyllabic verse, having misconceived the spirit of the latter altogether.(2)

In determining the true origin of the verse of the *Pater-noster* we have two alternatives: first, the familiar octosyllabic rhythm of the Latin hymns, and second the corresponding French verse. Both were well known to the English of the 12th century,—(though the particular translator of the *Pater-noster* is likely to have been more familiar with Latin hymns than with French romances). Of the two, the Latin verse was both accentual and syllabic, the French syllabic, but not in our sense accentual. The English verse, as Schipper clearly shows, is accentual but not syllabic; that is to say each verse contains four accents, but the number of syllables varies widely. Thus we find extreme examples in

>For alswa god hit bit, (27)

a verse of only 6 syllables, and

>Thi nome beo iblecced, thet we segged, (57)

a verse of 11 syllables. In other words, this verse presents no characteristic of the French verse;—but its

---

(1) pp. 89—100.
(2) Schipper, p. 107. See § 43, *ante*, for a discussion of his misconception.

chief peculiarity (i. e. its new, though still uniform number of accents), which distinguishes it from all earlier English verse, is found in the Latin, and there only.

This verse, it will be remembered, is earlier than that of *King Horn* It is governed by the essential principles of the decayed Old English hemistich, but the fixed number of accents has been changed from 2 to 4, —an extension suggested by the Latin. *King Horn* on the other hand, exhibits more fidelity to English tradition, clinging still, in theory, to the original two accents: but its tendency to verses of 3 or 4 actual accents assimilates it more or less closely to the *Pater-noster*, and in either of the poems many lines can be pointed out which might just as well have been introduced in the other.

The next developments of the four-accent verse need not be examined in detail. A number of specimens from the 13th and 14th centuries are discussed by Schipper.(1) They may be regarded as descendants of either the *Pater-noster* or *King Horn*. The uniform number of four accents might perhaps be regarded as a natural development from the latter, though of course the influence of the former explains it more obviously; but on the other hand such poems as the *Surtees Psalms* and *Handlyng Sinne* exhibit such freedom in the number of syllables that we cannot but recognize a strong native English spirit in them. The first-named, in particular, are decidedly looser in this respect than the *Pater-noster*, for in the latter the Latin influence was evidently felt as a check, though a feeble one.

Thus we find for this branch of the 4-accent verse of our English poetry a two-fold origin. On the one hand there was a direct imitation of the Latin verse ot the Ambrosian hymns, corrupted by English habit to a non-syllabic form: and on the other hand there was a

---

(1) p. 258, *et seq.*

native verse of two essential accents, so extended as to its number of syllables that it ultimately became confounded with the former. To the foreign element in the more modern forms of this verse we must undoubtedly assign precedence; but we must not ignore the native.

§ 50. *Chaucer.* The subsequent course of this verse is a fairly steady progress toward equalization of the number of syllables. Schipper attributes this progress to the influence of French verse, and this influence was unquestionably very great. The author of *Cursor Mundi* may have been as familiar with Latin models as with French, but when Chaucer was refining and perfecting the verse-form, he must be presumed to have had the French chiefly in his eye and ear, if not consciously in his mind. Here, however, we must be cautious in defining the foreign influence. Chaucer's French library was not made up of accentual verse. The *Roman de la Rose*, for example, which he knew as well as he knew any French poem, was of essentially the same verse-structure as the works of Chrestien, and the number of tonic syllables per verse might be 4, 3, or even only 2. But the rule of 4 accents was already established in the English verse: it was the strict limitation of the number of syllables, in the French form, that attracted Chaucer's attention. This limitation gave to French verse its smoothness, and it was this smoothness that Chaucer was seeking. A verse of 8 syllables and 4 accents, in English, will in general have an iambic movement;—and Chaucer's verse, inheriting the 4-accent character, and borrowing from France an approximate copy of the octosyllabic character, did attain this movement as no earlier verse had done:—but we must remember that this movement is not found in Chaucer's model. We may therefore sum up the whole history of our octosyllabic verse in this way:—we borrowed its number of accents from the Latin, but owing to the vitality of our own native traditions we at first borrowed nothing further: the syllabic character of the verse (so far as it has been imported at all), came in only gradually, against stubborn resistance:—and it came not directly from the Latin, but indirectly, through the French.(1)

The English 5-accent verse was developed much later than the shorter form. The earliest known specimens date only from the beginning of the 14th century, and the form was not definitely established till Chaucer's time.(2) Here again, the principles which we have established will prevent us from accepting Schipper's theory that this verse was a mere imitation of the French decasyllabic line. Our observations upon the unaccentual character of French verse need not be pushed further: but there is another feature of French decasyllabics that is altogether opposed to Schipper's theory,—namely the fixed cæsura. In the English verse there is no such thing: indeed there is no cæsura at all, in the French

---

(1) I have purposely avoided complicating the issue by a discussion of the accentual tendency shown in some of the Norman-French poetry. This of course was due to English influence, and it may well serve for purposes of illustration as a hypothetical connecting link between the French and the English. Its actual importance, however, seems to have been slight.

It should be noted, also, that the French influence had been considerable, before Chaucer's time, in other forms of verse beside the octosyllabic. It is apparent in the English Alexandrine as early as the beginning of the 13th century (Schipper, p. 113, *et seq*.). But we must again be on our guard, for this verse cannot be counted as an out-and-out imitation of the French. Its accentual character was English-Latin like that of the shorter verse:—the idea of increasing the 4 accents to 6 was natural enough, after the change from 2 to 4;—and the result was to make a verse roughly resembling the French Alexandrine. The latter afforded not the model, but at most two or three suggestive hints.

(2) Schipper, p. 436 *et seq*. I can see no reason for believing that any of the isolated specimens mentioned by Schipper were in Chaucer's mind when he wrote his *Legend of Good Women*.

sense of the word; for while most such verses in English have natural pauses after the 3rd, 4th, 5th, 6th or 7th syllable, such pauses are the almost necessary consequence of the verse-form, not one of its essential elements. Schipper relegates to a foot-note the suggestion that our heroic verse may have originated in a different way, either through an abridgement of the Alexandrine or through an extension of the 4-foot line. This is of course more nearly the true view, but it is entirely immaterial which of the last two explanations we hit upon. Accentual verses of 4, 6 and 7 feet were already familiar long before Chaucer's time. They exhibited a more or less regular alternation of arsis and thesis. To devise a verse which should be essentially the same in principle, but should have five accents instead of 4, 6 or 7, was a task that Chaucer's genius might well achieve unaided; and to call his product an *imitation* of a foreign verse built on entirely different principles, or even to call it specifically an abridgement of the Alexandrine or an extension of the shorter verse, seems almost a bit of supererogation.

§ 51. *The syllabic principle in modern English verse.* Our four-foot verse reached virtually its final stage of development under Chaucer's hands. Absolute syllabic regularity was not essential then, and it has never become so. Our five-foot verse, on the other hand, has taken one step further since Chaucer's time, and in its present form it affords some recognition—though feeble—to the syllabic principle.(1)

In the first place, while it now not infrequently runs beyond the number of 10 syllables, it never falls short

---

(1) The same thing might be asserted of the 4-foot verse; but, in view of the frequent employment of the *Penseroso* variety of this metre, such an assertion seems somewhat strained.

of that number.(1)   This rule is made the more striking by the freedom of our poets in the use of inversions, and verses occur which a Frenchman or even a German might easily regard as purely syllabic. Thus initial inversions are not only single, (a very common form, of course), but often double, as in

> Palpitated, her hand shook, and we heard
> *The Princess*, IV, 370.

and (much less frequently) even triple, as in

> Harmonizing silence without a sound
> *Epipsychidion* (near the end).

> Belus or Serapis their gods, or seat
> *Par. Lost.* I, 720.

> How the lit lake shines, a phosphoric sea(2)
> *Childe Harold*, III, 93.

When Tennyson wrote, in *The Coming of Arthur*,

> But Arthur, looking downward as he past,
> Felt the light of her eyes into his life
> Smite on the sudden,

he might without blame have written either

> Had felt the light of her eyes into his life

or

> Had felt the light of eyes into his life,

but he could not have written simply

> Felt the light of eyes into his life.

So, too, the famous line in *The Princess*

> And murmuring of innumerable bees,

would be correct with the *and* omitted, or with *murmuring* changed to *buzzing*:—but both changes could not be made together.

---

(1) A 9-syllable line in blank verse or heroic couplets would be regarded as either a bad line or an example of bold license. I have not noted any such line since the Elizabethan drama.

(2) Though in this verse many readers would perhaps emphasize *lake*.

There are perhaps two possible explanations of this avoidance of the 9-syllable line. It may be because the principle of syllabism must be respected, or it may be because a 9-syllable line would give a trochaic rather than iambic rhythm. A further consideration will show the insufficiency of the latter hypothesis more clearly: but in the meantime it may be remarked that trochaic rhythm does not necessarily result in a 9-syllable line. If, instead of the line quoted above from *Paradise Lost* we read

> Belus or Serapis, or to seat

the effect is certainly that of a series of trochees, with catalexis; but if for Shelley's line we substitute

> Harmonizing peace without a sound

the masculine cæsura still restores the iambic run in the latter part of the line.(1)

But the presence of the syllabic principle is shown clearly in the case of interior inversions, and conclusively in cases of postponement or entire omission of one of the normal five accents. As a single striking specimen of the former license, (which is of course very common), the following may serve:

> And dust shalt eat all the days of thy life.
> *Par. Lost*, X, 178.

The second class of cases includes all those verses which are commonly described as containing pyrrhics followed by spondees.(2) It is evident, however, as a few examples will show, that such a description, while satisfying the requirements of a mere catalogue, does not account scientifically for the rhythmical effect of the verses.

---

(1) Just as it has been observed that a masculine cæsura in quantitative hexameters gives an anapæstic run to the second hemistich. (Seymour, *Introduction to the Language and Verse of Homer*, § 40, p.)

(2) Cf. esp. J. B. Mayor, *Chapters on English Metre*.

Clench thine eyes now; 'tis the last instant, girl.
Rossetti, *Sonnets for Pictures*, II, 1.

The weight of the superincumbent hour
Adonais XXXII, 5.

And plunged all noiseless into the deep night.
Hyperion, I, 357.

That I may sit and pour out my sad sprite
The Faithful Shepherdess, IV, 4.

Then tore with bloody talon the rent plain
Childe Harold, III, 18.

The house-dog moans and the beams crack; nought else.
The Cenci, III, 2.

O'er the glad waters of the dark blue sea.
The Corsair, I, 1.

The line from *The Cenci*, for example, may be divided into feet as follows:

The house | -dog moans | and the | beams crack | nought else,

the 3rd foot being a pyrrhic and the 4th a spondee. But if it be compared with the following,

The house | -dog moans | and the beams | are cracked

it will be seen that the reading of the first four feet is exactly the same in the two cases, so far as time and stress are concerned. The latter line is in the familiar Christabel metre, and the 3rd foot is an anapæst:—so we see that the pyrrhic in the former line is not a foot at all, except to the eye. It seems doubtful wisdom, therefore, to try to reduce such verses to regularity by dividing them into dissyllabic feet at all. The better explanation is that while the postponement of the third accent is a variation from the normal, the strict observance of the syllabic rule keeps the verse within bounds.

The line from *The Corsair* may be read with 4, 5, or 6 stresses. Probably to some readers it will seem to have seven, of nearly equal weight; so that in a purely accentual metre, in which syllabic regularity was not regarded at all, it would be equivalent to

O'er the gladdened waters of the darkly billowed sea.

In any case, no division into equal feet can exhibit its real rhythm;—yet when the line is read with its context,

> O'er the glad waters of the dark blue sea,
> Our thoughts as boundless, and our souls as free, &c.

it is felt to be not merely beautiful in itself, but perfectly in accord with the general run of the heroic couplet. The reason is not that it has a certain number of feet or accents, but chiefly that it has exactly ten syllables.(1)

It seems, therefore, that when the syllabic system of the French impressed itself upon our poets, its effect was not merely to produce a more or less regular alternation of arsis and thesis, though of course its chief influence was of this indirect character. It seems that the syllabic system itself, as it exists in French poetry, is present in our own heroic verse, though it is but seldom clearly and unmistakably revealed. Our verse is of a very complex constitution, and any description based upon feet or accents alone, or on both together, is not adequate to cover all the phenomena. In general, it may be said that the verse may depart from syllabic regularity in certain respects, where the 5 accents are marked, or where the general iambic run is fairly apparent; but where this is not the case, the syllabic principle commonly comes in to save the uniformity of the metre.

It hardly needs to be pointed out that the final developments of this syllabic principle in English verse did not come at either of the two periods of French literary ascendency. The principle secured its foothold on English soil because of its own intrinsic value, and its fitness for our language. But its latest developments

---

(1) Interesting examples of Milton's usage have been collected by Robert Bridges. (*Milton's Prosody*, Oxford, 1893).

were facilitated by the impulse given to it in the early period of French influence, and however we may speculate as to what would have been, had that influence not existed, an account of the foreign sources of our versification would not be complete without mention of these latest phenomena.

www.ingramcontent.com/pod-product-compliance
Lightning Source LLC
Chambersburg PA
CBHW020142170426
43199CB00010B/854